THE ANARCHY OF FEELING

THE ANARCHY OF FEELING

Man's Struggle for Freedom and Maturity

ALEXANDER A. SCHNEIDERS

SHEED AND WARD – NEW YORK

© Sheed and Ward, Inc., 1963

Library of Congress Catalog Card Number 63–17136

Manufactured in the United States of America

To Dr. Joseph R. Stanton
Gentle Physician, Friend, and Healer
who made this book possible
by his priceless gift of time

FOREWORD

IN AN AGE of reason there is of course a strong tendency to deify the intellect and thus, paradoxically, to dehumanize man by an overemphasis of his distinctively human quality. The great minds of the past—Plato, Aristotle, Socrates, Augustine, Aquinas, Kant, Darwin, Einstein—themselves men of surpassing intellectual endowments, extolled the supremacy of the intellect in the affairs of men and even of the heart, and thus were apt to relegate human feelings and passion to a much lower level. Reason was king, and any attempt on the part of the feelings to gain control over the organization called man was regarded as anarchy and a "movement" to be put down as quickly and as expeditiously as possible. Intellect elevated man to the realm of the gods and gave him dominion over the baser elements in the kingdom of personality. The feelings and passions were regarded as unruly subjects over whom intellect had to exercise benevolent, if not despotic, control.

But Freud, the inventor of instinctual man, changed all this. He also dehumanized the human personality, but in his own distinctive way and in terms of his own genius. He saw man not as an organization over whom the intellect was king, but rather as a biological organism in whom the intellect is weak and ineffectual, and over whom instincts and feelings exercised despotic control. For Freud, the organization called man is essentially an anarchy governed by willful, dynamic, and uncontrolled forces that constantly threaten *dis*order and *dis*-organization.

It was Freud's genius to discover and to develop the portrait of instinctual man; but in so doing he opened up a Pandora's box of ideas and attitudes, of theories and speculations that have distorted our concept of the human mind, and have done a great deal to pave the way for the anarchy of feeling. Hence the aim of psychoanalysis or of psychotherapy is not to re-establish the dominion of the intellect; it is rather to unbridle the instincts and feelings for the sake of "spontaneity." The main task is not to get the patient to think for himself, but to abreact. The big question is not "What do you think?" but rather "How do you feel about this?"

This general attitude toward feeling as opposed to reason is reflected with startling clarity in the reactions and the lives of troubled people who seek help from counseling and psycho-therapy. Desperately, but often vainly, they search for the rule of reason which will free them from the anarchy of their own feelings. Too often they leave the counselor's chair or the analyst's couch with no more ability to control their rebellious and riotous feelings than when they started their tortuous route through the labyrinthine passages of the un-conscious. The intellect remains dethroned and they live their lives in an anarchy of feeling that robs them of any happiness, productivity, or contentment.

This book seeks to explore various aspects of this anarchy, not in the vain hope of discovering panaceas for the ravages of feeling, but of shedding some light on how feelings become despotic, and demonstrating the basic truth that where reason is king the feelings are subject to it.

The case studies used are real, but certain basic facts have been changed and disguised in such a way that no recognition or identification is possible. Perhaps through the strangulated efforts of these unfortunate people to find peace of mind, the reader himself will learn how better to overcome the anarchy of feeling.

ALEXANDER A. SCHNEIDERS

CONTENTS

CONTENTS

Thy hand, great Anarch! lets the curtain fall
And universal darkness buries all.

ALEXANDER POPE

THE ANARCHY OF FEELING

I THE REVOLT AGAINST REASON

*Wouldst thou subject all things to thyself? Then
subject thyself to thy reason.*

—SENECA.

EVERY THINKING PERSON today is aware of the tremendous
change and upheaval in human values and in our ways of
thinking about important things during the past one hundred
years. Some of this change is written up and even extolled as
progress, and certainly there has been a great deal of material
and economic advancement during this period. We have con-
quered distance and caused it to shrink to unbelievably small
proportions. We have pierced the almost impenetrable wall of
outer space and are even now threatening to carry our way
of life to the other hapless planets of the universe. We have
converted the contemporary kitchen into a haven of gadgetry
in which the refrigerator defrosts itself and the tin can can be
made to release its contents by electrical control. We have
emancipated modern woman from the home, from the nursery, and finally from herself. We have democratized education, and have made the college diploma available to additional
thousands of young men and women who in an earlier age
would have been content to graduate from grade school. We
have created an unbelievable network of paved highways that
reach into every corner of the land, and we have filled them
with millions of automobiles that represent a staggering invest-

ment of billions of dollars. We have raised the standard of living to much greater heights, so that more people have more things and more gadgets today than even a Jules Verne could have dreamed of a hundred years ago.

We have, in other words, created a utopia of sorts, but a utopia that has some essential ingredients missing. It makes us think of a house that is constructed of solid material things and cemented together with pleasure and convenience, but in which there is little human warmth or happiness. The automobiles glisten with brilliant color and purr like kittens; the gadgets are fun and give us the feeling of dominion over drudgery; mass education creates the illusion that we are really accomplishing something; and the penetration of outer space stimulates the added illusion that at last we are as free as the birds of the air.

But in the background one can discern a funereal dirge. There is a restless shifting of nations toward catastrophic war. There is too much hostility and hatred for anyone to feel a sense of security or peace. Too many persons carry with them a daily burden of fear and anxiety, and swell the coffers of liquor distillers in their desperate attempt to drown their tensions in a bottle. Too many people require counseling or psychotherapy to shore up their reserves so that they may do battle with reality. There are too many divorces and family breakdowns, and too many youngsters caught up in the viciousness of illicit sex, drinking, dope, and delinquency.

In brief, there are just too many defects in our mythical utopia to permit the complacent conviction that things are going well and we are making a great deal of progress. Progress and human development, unfortunately, cannot be counted in the coin of material advantages, the availability of weekend pleasure trips, or a raise in salary. The human psyche demands more than this for its nourishment and self-realization. It is not a machine that can be fed with gadgets and oiled with occasional drops of pleasure. It is a rational thing—or a spiritual one, if you wish to be more exact—that naturally yearns for a more substantial fare than either materialism or hedonism is prepared to offer. It simply cannot subsist on gadgets, money, pleasure, speed, or any of the other material things that contemporary man seems to feel are so important.

Just as the little child cannot subsist on bread alone, or comfort, or safety, but requires such basic ingredients as love, acceptance, and a sense of belonging for his psychic development to proceed in a normal, healthy manner, so modern man needs more than the security of the insurance policy, the speed of the automobile, or the pleasure of a cocktail party if he is to remain psychologically intact, or if he is to develop the resources that will help him ward off the devastating effects of conflict, anxiety, and guilt that threaten the destruction of his personal being. Whether we like it or not, man is primarily a rational being, and only secondarily a feeling being. This is not to minimize the importance of the feelings since we are quite aware of the role they play in enriching human life; but when feelings gain the ascendency, and are governed by the passionate urge for pleasure, reason is dethroned and the control which reason alone makes possible is thoroughly dissipated. Without this control man becomes a slave to the anarchy of feeling.

What has happened during the past one hundred years to change and to disrupt our value system, to emaciate our religious beliefs, and to pollute the stream of spiritual thought? In briefest form the answer is that the intellectual stalwarts of the past century successfully engineered a widespread revolt against reason. In a short space of time, reason was dethroned, and along with it psychological freedom and the deep, existential spirituality that psychic man needs if he is to cope successfully with the anxieties and threats, the stresses and strains of contemporary existence. In place of freedom man is offered a pallid, unworkable, and destructive determinism that insures the anarchy of feeling all of the power and scope it needs to destroy the individual person. In place of spiritual values that can enrich and strengthen the ego in its ceaseless battle with reality, man is offered the dry bread of a materialistic philosophy that clogs his system and hampers his efforts for survival. In place of perdurable moral and religious truths and principles, he is given a fleeting, hedonistic principle according to which pleasure is the be-all and end-all of existence. This is supposed to make materialism palatable, but it only serves to further clog the system and increase psychic inhibition because it is poorly suited to man's intrinsic rationality.

The leaders of this revolt against reason are easy to pick out. Any such roster would certainly include and almost certainly begin with Sigmund Freud, the apostle of sex and the expounder of modern hedonism. Then, of course, there was Charles Darwin, who convinced the world that the rationality of man could be explained away by the organicity of the brute. And there was the great psychologist, William James, who tried so hard to find the soul in a stream of consciousness but never quite succeeded in doing so. There was William McDougall, another of the great psychologists, who made the intellect of man into a servant of animal instincts, and who played havoc with man's freedom. And then there was John B. Watson, who, in his blind hatred of the soul and anything connected with it, threw out everything that was even remotely rational and spiritual in man. And finally, there was John Dewey, whose pragmatism put the final stamp of disapproval on man's nobler aspirations.

All of these men, you understand, were outstanding in their respective fields, and several of them reached the edge of greatness. To criticize some of their philosophical short-comings is not to deny the entire product of their particular genius. It would be foolish to ignore or belittle the contributions that Freud made to our understanding of the human mind and its dynamics. Without Freud, and his remarkable insights into what goes on in the deeper recesses of the unconscious, and how this affects the ideas and feelings, the decisions and aspirations of the human person, we would be seriously handicapped in trying to understand our fellow human beings and our clients, and even more handicapped in our efforts to cope therapeutically with human problems. Without William James, and his *Principles of Psychology*, and his equally enriching *Varieties of Religious Experience*, our understanding of certain psychological and religious phenomena would be much poorer, and psychology itself would have been deprived of its greatest champion.

We may not agree with William McDougall and his untiring insistence on the primacy of the instincts, but we would have to admit that the science of psychology is richer for his having been a part of it. His theory of the instincts, as propounded in his unusually successful book, *Social Psychology*, is still worthy of careful consideration today. We may scorn the straight-jacket of materialism with which John Watson bound psychology in the early years of this century, but we would have to concede that he did much good in clearing the psychological atmosphere of numerous confusions and ambiguities. These men were outstanding pioneers, leaders, and designers of unique or at least stimulating systems of thought.

They were pathfinders in a jungle of misconceptions who led the way to a better understanding of the human mind.

But we cannot blink away the fact that sometimes the paths they laid out led nowhere, and at other times led us deeper into the jungle of misunderstanding. In their tracking of the unknown, these pioneers, too, could get lost; and certainly, if the contemporary counter-revolt against the dethronement of reason is any indication, we can assume that they did get lost a number of times in their efforts to explore the makeup of the human mind. We see this fact rather clearly exemplified in the changed attitude toward human freedom, rationality, and moral responsibility among psychologists as well as psychiatrists and psychotherapists. We see it also in the modifications of psychoanalysis that have occurred during the past thirty years, and in some of the newer approaches to counseling and psychotherapy. These developments are of course part of the counter-revolt, and they bid fair to play an important part in restoring the functional significance of the intellect and in dethroning the anarchy of feeling. In this connection we think immediately of such persons as Karen Horney, Erich Fromm, Harry Stack Sullivan, Carl Rogers, Gordon Allport, Albert Ellis, and O. Hobart Mowrer who stand out prominently as apostles of a viewpoint which recognizes that material things and sensory pleasures are not the primary determinants of the good life.

Perhaps the greatest distortion in creating the anarchy of feeling is the hedonistic viewpoint that pleasure is the primary, if not the sole, determinant of human behavior. Pleasure, said Freud, is so predominant in the dynamics of conduct that it should be elevated to the status of a primary principle, and this of course is exactly what he did. The dynamic and philosophical viewpoint that pleasure is the goal of all behavior not only distorts the whole psychology of human motivation, but it sets the stage for a true anarchy of feeling. It is a simple matter to argue from the primacy of pleasure to the complete and unequivocal dominion of feeling, since pleasure is itself a feeling state. And certainly there are many persons whose own unique anarchy of feeling consists in a complete obeisance to Bacchus, the recognized supreme ruler of the domain of pleasure. Their god is their belly, pleasure is their goal, and the realm of eternal values or principles has no meaning whatever for them.

This particular anarchy of feeling has a close kinship with other types that we encounter in clients who seek counseling or psychotherapy. The dominion of pleasure over the lives of some people is quite common and is not recognized as any form of mental aberration; on the other hand, the dominion of feelings like hostility, hatred, inferiority, or guilt is recognized as a facet of the neurotic structure. However, it must be recognized that the person who suppresses reason and the spiritual values associated with it in favor of the lusts provided by pure pleasure-seeking is skating on thin ice if he hopes to maintain normality or mental health. Pleasure is not bad, or sinful, or destructive in itself, since it is an important part of human experience. But the unlicensed pursuit of pleasure coupled with the dethronement of reason and spiritual values must inevitably lead to personal dissolution. Freud, therefore, contributed a great deal to the anarchy of feeling by his unremitting emphasis on the importance and value of pleasure to the dynamics of human conduct.

William James, and after him Dewey, also contributed to the dethronement of reason, but in a totally different way. James had a great deal of difficulty with the concept of the spiritual soul and thus ended up with the stream of conscious-

ness theory and a philosophy of pragmatism. For his part,
Dewey took up the latter part of James' thinking and converted it into a philosophy of education. It is this pragmatic
philosophy that tends to support the revolt against reason and
indirectly the anarchy of feeling. The basic law of pragmatism
is usefulness, and thus things are to be judged not in terms
of reasonableness, intrinsic value, or objective principles, but
by the extent to which they contribute to the practical neces-
sities of everyday living. From this viewpoint gadgets and
time-savers, automobiles and dishwashers, education and marriage assume a new dimension, and are evaluated in terms of
practical utility. Thus it is not practical for the housewife to
tolerate the drudgeries of creating a home, of giving up a
career, of having children, of sacrificing for the sake of the
family, or of doing without the luxuries of two cars, an
expensive vacation, money in the bank, or a split-level home.
It is much more practical for the wife to keep her job and
hire a stranger to care for the children, or, better still, not to
have children at all. It is more practical to eat out than go
through the drudgery of preparing a meal. It is more practical
to have two cars so that no one will be hampered getting to
and from work. And so on through a whole litany of rationalizations that start with a pragmatic attitude.

  This pragmatic attitude plays host to the anarchy of feeling
with very little difficulty. If practicality rather than principle
is to determine our behavior, we are but one step away from
the dominion of feeling or pleasure. Where reason is dethroned in favor of utility, feeling is bound to take over. To
say "I don't feel like it" is very similar in the psychological
order to saying "It's not practical." The pragmatist, like the
out-and-out hedonist, gives homage to the senses, because
reason makes far too many demands. Pragmatism, hedonism,

and the anarchy of feeling may seem to be strange bed-fellows, but they keep each other warm and comfortable.

In similar vein, the materialism of Watson and the instinctualism of McDougall contributed to the dethronement of reason. It is obvious to anyone acquainted with the trappings of the human mind that instincts are dominated by pleasure, and thus are blood-brothers to the feelings and emotions. McDougall's reduction of the intellect to the service of the instincts is a quick road to the anarchy of feeling. By the same rule, in the philosophy of materialism we find able support for the doctrines of pleasure and practicality. If nothing exists but matter, and the soul is a fiction of the philosophers, then certainly the instincts are king and the intellect is a concept devoid of meaning. This is one of the most striking examples of the revolt against reason; and it certainly plays a leading role in the enthronement of feeling. It is this philosophy of materialism that dominates the thinking of many people in contemporary society. Everywhere we turn we see evidence of this shabby and arid philosophy. Billboards, books, magazines, radio, and television ceaselesssly proclaim the gospel of material gratification. Under the barrage of this propagandizing, the hapless individual quickly succumbs, and the anarchy of feeling is given an additional boost.

You understand, of course, that the dethronement of reason brought about by the advancement of a materialistic, hedonistic, and pragmatic philosophy is not the same thing as the shackling of reason that is caused by extreme anxiety or a neurotic process. Let us realize that the dethronement of reason was at first philosophical and historical and only later appeared in its psychological form. The unseating of reason and the anarchy of feeling in the severe neurotic is a psychological parallel to the philosophical dethronement of reason during the era of the great psychological discoveries.

This parallel is very real and deserves the closest scrutiny. In the matter of freedom, for example, the revolt against reason led ineluctably to psychological determinism, in the course of which materialism, hedonism, and pragmatism played distinctive roles. And just as these dehumanizing philosophies worked to unhinge and then destroy psychological freedom as a useful concept, so too does the neurotic pattern unhinge and destroy freedom in its unhappy victim.

The undermining of the concept of freedom is an invariable concomitant of the anarchy of feeling, and each one of the psychological protagonists whom we have mentioned contributed to its demise. We realize, of course, that psychological determinism as a philosophical viewpoint will not of itself generate a neurosis; but it is important to understand that such thinking can and does undermine people's belief in their own mastery or self-determination. The philosopher's statement that there is no freedom sounds strangely like the complaint of the neurotic that he has no control over his thoughts or feelings. The one statement comes from a philosophical conviction of man's weaknesses; the other from a neurotic conviction of personal weakness. In any event, both convictions pay homage to the anarchy of feeling. One could turn this around and say that it is the dominion of feeling that dethrones reason and sets a limit on personal freedom; but it is just as logical to argue that the loss of personal freedom is a basic determinant of the anarchy of feeling. In subsequent chapters we will see many instances of this relationship, and in each case the one element is complementary to the other.

The dethronement of reason, then, takes two forms—the one, a philosophical attack based on the tenets of materialism, pragmatism, hedonism, and determinism; the other, an attack that grows out of the neurotic approach to life. We have said enough about the philosophical revolt against reason; our principal efforts from now on will be directed toward the problems engendered by the dethronement of reason and the loss of freedom exemplified in the lives of so many unhappy and neurotic persons.

What is this anarchy of feeling as it exists in the individual person, and how does it work? What is its relationship to rationality and psychological freedom? You are aware, of course, that feelings and emotions, even the most powerful ones, are in themselves natural responses to varying stimuli and situations, which not only contribute a great deal to the dynamics of behavior but also enrich our lives in a way that no other response can. Life would be very drab without love, pleasure, excitement, wonder, and similar feeling states. Even the more disruptive feelings like anger and fear play an important part in energizing our responses.

But it is true that emotions can easily get out of hand and cause an explosion within the personality that leads to the disorganization of both thinking and behavior. When anger boils into rage, and fear leaps into panic, consciousness is blurred, judgment becomes warped, and behavior may become completely disrupted. Even love, as we shall see in the next chapter, can become an anarchy of feeling. Worse still, there are many derivatives of natural feelings that are in themselves detrimental to mental health. Anger may be disruptive, but it does serve a useful purpose; whereas hostility and hatred are of themselves damaging to the personality and will act to destroy interpersonal relationships. Love ennobles the human mind, but jealousy only works to destroy it. To be humble is virtuous, but to feel inferior is to court a great deal of psychic trouble. All such feelings, including anxiety, guilt, insecurity, inferiority, and like processes, are inimical to psychological health and tend to weaken or to destroy human relationships.

In order to maintain psychological health, it is necessary for us to retain dominion over our feelings and emotions. We cannot afford to become their victims or slaves unless we are willing to tolerate an anarchy of feeling within ourselves. The enthronement of feeling necessarily involves the dethronement of reason, and reason is the only source of control or mastery of our different reactions. It is reason that forms the groundwork of psychological freedom, which is nothing but the capacity of the human mind to initiate, and exercise some control over, various responses. When feelings achieve overwhelming power, and especially when they combine in such a way as to reinforce each other, freedom declines and the resulting state of affairs can best be described as an anarchy. It is this personal revolt against reason, this anarchy of feeling, that we wish to examine more fully in the following pages. We shall see again and again what happens when reason is dethroned and feeling takes control of the personality. We will attempt to lay bare the causes and background of these neurotic conditions in the hope that you, the reader, will acquire a better understanding of them.

2 THE TYRANNY OF LOVE

What is mature love? It is union under the condition
of preserving one's integrity, one's individuality. . . .
In love the paradox occurs that two beings become
one and yet remain two.

—ERICH FROMM, *The Art of Loving.**

WE HEAR a great deal nowadays about love. Love is the great redeemer of human relationships, the one force that can solve the problems of mankind. It is the savior of the marital union, the force that binds man to God, and even the intangible link between counselor and client that initiates and sustains the healing process. Even Freud, who emphasized unceasingly the powers of sex and lust, is credited with the rediscovery of love. In the therapy room and in the pulpit, in countless articles and books, we are constantly reminded of the redemptive power of love; and because we are always on the search for a simple formula and a soothing panacea that will solve all of our problems, we swallow these platitudes greedily without any mastication whatever. In many instances we see no connection between the platitudes that we have gulped down and the resulting indigestion.

This love potion assumes many forms, and sometimes it is so disguised as to be unrecognizable. One of the more favorite disguises is what one inventive genius called "togetherness," a concept that is so oversweetened with sentimentality that

* New York: Harper & Row, Publishers, Inc., 1956.

even its devotees are beginning to regurgitate it. Togetherness, hailed by its advocates as a sign of imperishable love, is a striking instance of the tyranny of love. It is also a particularly obnoxious instance of the anarchy of feeling. I remember talking to a young couple, married ten years and with six children, at a marriage conference some months ago in which the wife proudly asserted that she and her husband had never been separated for even the shortest period of time, and that they did everything together. The husband affirmed this gluelike relationship with all the vigor of his young manhood. In fact, he became quite vociferous about it and angrily rejected my plea for individuality. In a very brief time he became manifestly hostile; but, fortunately for him and his passive, dependent wife, he did not recognize that the hostility toward me was nothing more than a displacement of the anger he felt toward a clinging, dependent wife.

The quality of togetherness, when carried to an extreme in the name of love, clearly indicates the tyrannical extremes to which love can go. One of man's greatest prerogatives, and an inherent right, is the quality of *individuality*. This individuality, incidentally, stems directly from the fact of man's rational nature. Other things in nature—the birds and the bees, for example,—are individual; but man alone has the kind of individuality that becomes *personalized* by reason of the capacity to make judgments and decisions. Human individuality, and therefore personality, becomes debilitated by a tooclose dependency. Is there anything more disturbing than the picture of a weak, passive husband "yessing" every one of his wife's demands? We instinctively feel that the husband especially should exercise his right to individual judgment even though both of them always strive for agreement on essential matters. I know one husband who goes to the same resort every year and hates every minute of it; when you realize that he has been doing this for twenty-five years, you can imagine how he feels toward his demanding wife.

There is, of course, nothing wrong with love when it is handled correctly; and this can be said of all human emotions, except those that are inherently negative in character. It is love carried to the extreme of *possession*, and love that is allowed to blind the intellect and to fetter judgment, that establishes tyranny over human behavior. In such instances the anarchy of feeling stands out in sharp contrast to the dominion of intelligence.

In twenty years of marriage counseling I have seen numerous instances of couples, young and old, who loved each other and yet found it impossible to work out a happy marital relationship. In some instances their love ran so deep that they were willing to tolerate the incessant, destructive conflict that raged between them day and night, and that despoiled whatever children they brought into the world. How often we hear it said that "Jim and I are still very much in love; but the divorce must go through. We simply cannot seem to get along together." One such couple that I had in counseling for a number of months could not stem the tide of conflict long enough to get through a forty-five-minute session. These two love-birds could not be together in any circumstances without raging at each other about trivialities, calling each other names, and generally making life miserable for themselves and the people around them.

Is this the tyranny of love, or should we say rather that some people are psychologically incompatible? The answer lies in the fact that in most instances of marital strife and incompatibility both spouses are well liked and accepted by business acquaintances, friends, and relatives, who characteristically find it impossible to understand why these two fine people don't get along together. True, this kind of love is not of the best variety; but it is the fact that such a relationship exists that touches off the conflict.

We see the tyranny of love reflected in the distressingly large number of divorces and separations each year, in the pain and unhappiness of mixed marriages, in the sordid squabbles over children and the best way to raise them, and in many similar situations. I have never met a couple in marriage counseling who did not protest that they loved each other very much when they were courting and when they got married. But when you ask the young couple of different religious backgrounds, for example, whether they were aware of the difficulties that would be encountered once they were married, the answer invariably comes back, "Yes, we knew that there would be difficulties, but we were sure that love would transcend all."

Herein lies the tyranny of an emotion like love. It really clouds consciousness and blinds the intellect. It can spawn the most immature type of judgment and lead to the most violent kind of behavior. In a recent newspaper there was the story of a man who hired for murder. Why? Because he wanted to eliminate the husband whose wife he had fallen in love with, and who was reluctant to grant her a divorce. Four hundred thousand divorces each year are glaring testimony to the poor judgments made under the tyranny of love. Here again we can see how the anarchy of feeling can impair human thinking and lead to the total disintegration of human relationships.

Nowhere is the tyranny of love more strikingly manifested than in the relationship between parents and children. It appears in many different forms, most of which are destructive of personality development and of wholesome relationships.

There is, for example, the practice of over-indulgence, as well as the practice of over-protection. There are the parental errors of possessiveness, jealousy, favoritism, cross-identification, and similar failures in the development of parent-child relationships. In all these relationships the element of love is clearly discernible, and plays its part in wreaking havoc just as it does in togetherness, in marital relationships, and in other human situations.

Let us pause for a moment and ask what happens in these feeling-dominated situations. Why is it that love, which has such great potentiality for bettering human relationships and promoting healthy growth, can produce such deleterious effects? Like all feelings and drives, the emotion of love influences and tends to distort the perceptual process, just as it tends to distort judgment. When love enters the picture, we no longer see the object of love in sharply-defined realistic tones. This is clearly illustrated by the doting parent who looks at her ugly child and gurgles something to the effect of how cute he is. Everybody else, not influenced by this feeling toward the child, thinks he looks like a monster.

The same thing happens, of course, when a young man falls in love. In these instances we have what the psychologist would call a "reorganization of the psychological field," which is a high-flown phrase for expressing the fact that the fellow can't see straight. This is how a powerful feeling like love can establish a tyranny over other conscious functions. A person looking in a mirror, presumably in love with himself, never sees what other people see who have the advantage of objectivity. This has a redeeming quality because it often keeps us from despising ourselves. In all such instances our perceptions, as well as our ideas and judgments, are distorted according to what we want to believe is true.

This distortion also affects our behavior and our relationships with others when we are under the influence of a powerful emotion. For example, every parent, in his saner moments, knows perfectly well that over-indulgence and over-protection of a child are detrimental to his personal growth. It is obvious to everyone that spoiling a child makes him selfish, weakens his personality structure, and causes him to be generally obnoxious. Yet parents will invariably plead innocent to any charge of mishandling on the ground that they love the child and just can't help giving him what he wants. Grandparents are notorious for the commission of this crime against children, but the difference is that grandparents gleefully admit their guilt because it is the first time, as parents, that they have been able to smother a child with love without the deep sense of responsibility that parents have for the welfare of the child.

In the grave error of over-protection we see another glaring instance of the tyranny of love reaching into the basic structure of the child's personality. The over-protected child is quite easy to identify when he reaches adulthood. He is the anxious, timid, insecure, uncertain, and unconfident person who is paralyzed by the thought of adult responsibilities, and who shrinks from the overpowering task of making decisions. Like the clinging housewife we made reference to a few pages back, he is lacking in strong self-identity, in independence, and in the self-assurance necessary to cope with the realities of adult living.

Children must of course be protected, especially when they are very young. But the over-protective mother, in the zeal generated by the flame of love, insists on standing between the child and reality, and thus never gives him an opportunity to test reality, to find out what it is like, to act independently, to make his own judgments, and to come to grips with responsibility. It is only by thrusting the child, and especially the adolescent, into real situations and letting him "sink or swim" that he learns how to cope with them. The capacity to be decisive is learned only by making decisions. The willingness to reach for and to accept responsibilities, and then do something about them, can only come through the experience of handling responsibilities.

Real, day-by-day living involves a great many mistakes, failures, errors in judgment, reverses, disappointments, and heartaches. The child must learn that this is so, and how to "ride with the punch" when these things occur. He must learn how to accept and to assimilate his own mistakes and failures, and how to profit from them. Unfortunately, the over-protective parent forbids this type of experience to her beloved child. Frozen by her own anxieties, and goaded by her feeling for the child, she walks constantly by his side to see that "nothing happens to him." And that is just the kind of an outcome we can expect. Nothing will happen to him—not even personality growth. Look about you among your friends and neighbors, or maybe even in your own home. You will see how the tyranny of love spawns weakness, anxiety, emotional dependency, and immaturity.

Still another aspect of the tyranny of love is exemplified in the attitudes of *jealousy* and *favoritism*, which may certainly be regarded as two of the most damaging influences in the lives of children. Favoritism is particularly repugnant because it is a two-edged sword. Where the recipient is concerned, favoritism works very much like over-indulgence, and often with strikingly similar effects. The favored child may enjoy the special attention, the added affection, and the other good things that result from favoritism; but at the same time there is a strong likelihood that he will become self-centered, and develop the dangerous illusion that he is something special. In other instances, as often happens with over-indulgence, the child may become suspicious of the parent's motives, so that the favoritism produces exactly the opposite effect from what was expected. Instead, therefore, of breeding love, as the parent foolishly hopes, favoritism often breeds rejection, hostility, and distrust.

The more destructive effects of this distortion of love are seen in the child who is *not* favored, the one who must feel that he is lacking in those qualities possessed by the favored child, and is thus not as lovable, as worthy, or as wanted as others. How often neurotic adults complain that deep within themselves they feel so unworthy, so unwanted, or so basically evil! When we tear away the veil of time and get at the sources of these feelings, we invariably find an unloving, rejecting parent who, in a distorted application of love, had chosen another child as her favorite.

A particular aspect of favoritism, and one that can be just as damaging, is the relationship of *cross-identification*, which means simply that the father of the family is especially enamored of his daughter (or vice versa), and that the mother has a particularly soft spot in her heart for her son. As you can see, this is a special variety of favoritism, but one that can have even more serious consequences. You can imagine how a son must feel if the father is particularly solicitous for the affection and welfare of his "beautiful daughter." And a daughter won't feel any better if the mother's affection gravitates toward the son. But even worse than these feelings is the blight which such favoritism often brings to the growing personality of the boy or girl. Cross-identification can cause a great deal of anxiety and guilt, and always threatens to undermine the growth of a healthy self-identity. Tomboys are made out of this sort of stuff, and sometimes tomboys never grow up to be real women. Effeminacy in boys also reflects this inadequate identification. For boys to become men, and for girls to become women, it is important that they be given every opportunity to identify with the member of the same sex, that is, the boy with the father, and the girl with the mother. Otherwise, the eventual outcome is likely to include poor psychosexual development, sexual confusion, and widespread failure to develop adult roles in which manhood and womanhood are basic characteristics.

A particularly vicious and self-destructive aspect of the tyranny of love is the *feeling of jealousy* which plays a stellar role in the anarchy of feeling. There is no greater distortion of love than this vicious and dangerous emotion which perhaps has led to more sorrow and heart-break, and often to more violence, than any other single emotion. While jealousy derives from the relationship of love, it is compounded essentially of three powerful emotions, anger, fear, and hate. It is this amalgam of feeling which makes jealousy a dangerous emotion.

Let us consider two particularly disagreeable examples of jealousy, (1) the jealousy that a girl or a wife feels with respect to the man with whom she is in love; and (2) the jealousy that a parent feels with respect to a child who is claiming the attention and affection of the other parent. All of us have witnessed the destructive effects of the first type. Every time the male partner looks at another woman, is courteous and polite to members of the opposite sex, or in any way remotely suggests the possibility of interest or attraction, the feeling of jealousy begins to rage in the mind and heart of the wife or fiancée. Secretaries, professional colleagues, and anyone of the opposite sex within the neighborhood of the male "who belongs to me" can become the object of this crippling emotion. And what does jealousy do? Does it sweeten the relationship between the married couple in question? Does it promote the high purpose of love? Does it protect the jealous wife from the possible advances of the more "eager" members of her sex? On the contrary, jealousy undermines the relationship of love and eats into and destroys the emotional fiber of the jealous person.

I am reminded of the case of a very attractive married woman who, in her own words, "loved her husband very much." At the present writing, they have been married fourteen years and have a boy twelve years of age. The ink was not yet dry on the marriage certificate before the young wife began to let her husband know in unmistakable terms that she was extremely jealous and would not tolerate the least departure from her norms of correct marital behavior and conjugal devotion. There is no need to continue this unhappy story. Today, still attractive and young-looking, this wife is a lonely, broken-hearted, and deserted mother. After about two years of her jealous rages, the husband began to find his satisfaction in other places that were free of the raging destructiveness of jealousy. Today he cannot tolerate his wife, either as a companion or as a sexual partner. At the present moment, this unfortunate couple are seeking a separation.

The tyranny of love, as we have seen, is manifested in many different ways and with distressing effects on the personalities of the people involved. But we have reserved for our final analysis the most destructive of all aspects of this tyranny, and that is *possessive love*. In working with people of all ages and types, as school counselor and psychotherapist, I have seen countless instances of the deep ravages which this kind of love produces. It has a vampire-like quality which seems to suck the very marrow of personality from the unfortunate victim. As in other instances of "possession," the possessor in this case develops a parasitic hold on the personality of the loved object, and manages to permeate every aspect of the person's psychological and emotional being. In time the relationship becomes a symbiotic one, which precludes separation of the two persons involved, with the result that any real or significant individuality is made impossible, and relationships with others (particularly a relationship of love) are very poorly developed or even non-existent.

In order to grasp better the character of possessive love, let us consider briefly the case of a young woman, twenty-eight years old, who at the present time is a teacher of English in a public high school. This young woman, whom we shall call Betty, is the oldest of three children. She has a younger brother and a younger sister, both of whom are living, and both of whom have been under psychiatric treatment. The sister is married and has one child; the brother is intermittently employed as a music teacher. The mother and father are still living, and Betty visits them occasionally in a somewhat desultory effort to maintain, or perhaps to recapture, relationships that have always been tenuous in character.

Betty is a comely girl, who dresses rather well, communicates adequately in a counseling situation, and has managed to achieve some success in her chosen profession of teaching. However, she has a hangdog appearance which expresses itself in a lowering of the head so that the gaze is always upward, and a whiney voice that has worn thin through countless repetitions of personal complaints. When Betty says she feels good, it sounds like a suicide note. She complains of feelings of guilt that make her feel dirty and degraded; of repeated compulsions to wash her hands; of the sense of contamination; of the fear of death because of her badness; of the failure of God to answer her prayers; of not having a husband and children; of endless years of guilt and depression; and of countless other torments that have made of her life a continuous nightmare of almost intolerable experiences.

Before we try to find out what happened to Betty, let's ask what is fundamentally wrong with her. Certainly, she is an outstanding example of the anarchy of feeling, and never tires of repeating that she "doesn't *feel* good." Or that, no matter what the objective situation is, her *feelings* will not give her any peace of mind. Even though she knows *why* she feels guilty, and that it has nothing to do with wrong behavior, her feelings still maintain a stranglehold on her reason, and thus deny her the freedom that she desperately needs to become a real person.

This domination of feeling intrudes on Betty's thinking, her judgments and decisions, her behavior, and her relationships with other people. Even though she knows that it is not wrong to experience the natural urge to void bodily waste products, she will nevertheless feel guilty about such urges in certain situations. Thus, in the presence of other people or in Church, she will feel that this is wrong and will allow her behavior to be dictated by this feeling. When she goes to the bathroom, she must wash her hands repeatedly because she feels sure that they have been contaminated, and that this contamination will spread to other things, such as dishes and food. When this happens, she must then compulsively scrub the dishes until she is absolutely sure that all possibilities of contamination have been effectively removed.

Similarly, her relationships with other persons, while often on a friendly basis, are never deep, intimate, or lasting. She has never been in love with anyone, nor has she succeeded in winning anyone's love. She has an obsessive fear of sex, and is constantly plagued by a scrupulosity that revolves around books, newspapers, movies, magazines, and other media of communication that in any way advert to sexual realities. Thus, in every area of Betty's life, the tyranny of love has wrought its destructive influence, leaving her an unhappy, passive, and deeply neurotic person with a shadowy personality that precludes the development of wholesome, enriching, human relationships.

How did this unhappy girl get this way? What sort of pathology do we find when we study her background as an infant, child, and adolescent? Were her parents mean, ornery, punitive, rejecting, sadistic, or hostile? Not at all. It is true that the father was an inadequate, passive man who had an ugliness about him that repelled the children. But the father was not the stronger determinant of the children's developing personalities. It was the mother who was not any of the things we mentioned a moment ago. She saw herself as a devoted, loving parent whose children were the most important part of her life. And even today, Betty will say that she is sure that her mother loved her very much.

But the difficulty is that Mrs. X (Betty's mother), because of her own neurotic inadequacies, did not know how to apply the strength of love to her children. In her clumsy attempts to apply what love she was capable of, she grew to possess her children, and in the process devoured them. She constantly reminded them of things they ought to do; she was with them even when they were separated; she was mawkishly over-solicitous, over-protective and over-affectionate. Herself an extremely anxious person, she imparted extreme anxiety to Betty and her siblings. Each morning they had to go through

a ritual of examination and inspection that became excruciat-
ingly painful, and is still resented at the present time. In a
word, Mrs. X lived her children's lives, and thus they had no
chance at a life of their own.

Under such conditions, there is very little ego development,
and thus no real resources to cope with the demands of reality
or of self. In such persons the ego or self is like a thread of
taffy that dissolves very quickly when you pour warm water
over it. It has no fiber, no strength, and no resources with
which to battle against the forces within oneself or in the
world. Naturally, sex-identity is poor, and self-identity fundamentally weakened, so that human relationships, and the expression of basic needs, are very inadequate. We must remember that the development of genuine human relationships, and
the healthy gratification of basic needs and desires, can only
occur when the human personality has a hard core of selfhood. Only when we know what we are, who we are, and
where we are going, and thus have a firm and steady belief
in ourselves, can we maintain a firm grip on life, and plunge
unafraid into the realities and responsibilities of daily living.
This is what Betty lacks; and this is what her possessive, cloy-
ing mother failed to give her because she used love as a weapon
of tyranny instead of a vessel of goodness.

What are we to say about these distortions of love, these
tyrannies in which love is used to bludgeon a loved one into
submission, a crippling dependency, or a selfless vegetation?
Many readers will say that I am not talking about love at all,
but some horrible caricature of love. Love, they will say, is
understanding, kind, and good. It is an enrichment of the
spirit and a fulfillment of the promises that people make to
each other. Love is a mother's imperishable gift to her child,
and the husband's undying commitment to his wife. Love is

charity and friendliness and compassion. It is God's will working in the minds of men, and men's wills striving to possess
God. Love is not jealousy, or hatred, or possessiveness, or
anger, or fear, or favoritism. Love excludes all these things;
and thus the tyranny of love is a misleading term, and we
should call it something else.

What we have just said about love is certainly true. But the
simple fact of the matter is that all human emotions have
within themselves the seeds of tyranny, just as all government
has within itself the seeds of anarchy. There is no doubt in
the world that Betty's mother loved her, and that because
of this love, which became possessive, Betty is today an emotional cripple. No one can question the fact that the jealous
wife loves her husband, and that this jealousy springs from
the relationship of love. These are instances of love that has
become tyrannical, just as fear, or anger, or independence can
become tyrannical. Man's emotions are an important part of
his natural equipment and without them life would be a drab
and uninteresting affair. But the emotions are like a surgeon's
scalpel, which can be used to cut and to cure, but also to
destroy. The emotions—especially powerful ones like love—
must be held in balance. They must be brought under a system of controls and kept under the rule of man's more noble
faculties. If emotions are allowed to run amuck, reason is
quickly dethroned and the behavior of man degenerates into
childishness, infantilism, or beastiality. In such instances the
tryanny of love becomes a true anarchy of feeling.

3 SEX WITHOUT GUILT

Sensuality is the grave of the soul.

—CHANNING.

RUTH WAS a very pretty girl. Twenty-three or twenty-four years of age, she looked nineteen. And like many girls caught in the maelstrom of sexual promiscuity she was not only good-looking but very attractive. Everything about her, including the perfume that sent out its feelers in every direction, suggested seductiveness.

She looked at me for a long while and then said, "It was not my idea, coming here to see you. It was my folks' idea. They spoke to the parish priest about me and he had heard of your work with married couples. As far as I'm concerned, it's much ado about nothing."

"You mention a priest. Are you Catholic?"

"Oh, yes. I was baptized a Catholic, and attended only Catholic schools right through high school. I have been a practicing Catholic all my life. That is, until recently."

"Until recently?"

"Well, yes. You see, that's the reason I'm here. I was married in the Church a short time ago and I ran into some difficulties. Would you like to hear about them? It's not a very pretty story."

I said, "In this business we hear a lot of stories that aren't particularly pretty. Human nature being what it is, and counseling being concerned with human problems and weaknesses, we are bound to hear a lot of stories of suffering and unhappiness. Why don't you just tell me in your own words what the problem is?"

"Well, as I told you, I was married just a few months ago, and on my wedding day I slipped away on the pretext of being extremely tired, and spent some time in the apartment of a man whom I knew before I got married. In fact, to put it bluntly, we had sexual relationships. That's pretty crummy, isn't it?"

In twenty-five years of counseling and psychotherapy, involving scores of cases that revolved around sexual and marital difficulties, I had never encountered anything quite like this. I had worked extensively with promiscuous single men and women; with habitual masturbators; with homosexuals caught in a web of sexual behavior so bizarre and distorted as to tax human credulity; with distortions of sexual impulse that would make Krafft-Ebing want to revise his famous text; and with errant husbands and wives who found their neighbor's mate more interesting than their own, or who prowled the bistros of Chicago's Loop, or the Village in New York in an incessant, compulsive search for sexual adventures. But this was the first time that I had encountered the phenomenon of sexual promiscuity—that is, sex without guilt—asserting itself on the victim's wedding day.

I suppose that I showed some of the surprise in my face because the young lady, looking directly at me and without flinching so much as an eyebrow, said, "Did I shock you, Doctor? I thought you fellows had heard everything."

I said as nonchalantly as possible, "Would you like to tell me about it? I am sure that the details surrounding your behavior will shed considerable light on the problem."

Here, then, is the problem of sexual promiscuity, of sex without guilt. It is the problem of satyriasis and of nymphomania, the tragic story of the wanderers in the sexual wasteland who roam about in an endless and seemingly tireless search for sexual excitement and gratification. On the face of it, this would seem to be the anarchy of feeling in reverse—wherein the absence of feeling rather than its presence seems to lead to behavior distortion. But, as we shall see, this is a delusion. The promiscule—if we may coin a term—and the nymphomaniac are characterized very often by a diminished or inactive sense of guilt. Their countless violations of moral codes and principles relating to sex behavior have dulled their moral sensibilities to the point where guilt no longer counts as a regulating force in the organization of moral behavior. As someone once said about evil, "First, we are repelled by it; then we are attracted by it; then we embrace it." And this seems to be the rather sordid story of the sexual libertine. That is why we have called this chapter "Sex Without Guilt."

The absence of guilt, then, has quite a bit to do with the excessive and often perverted behavior of the sexual libertine. But the mere absence of feelings of guilt would not be enough of itself to explain the behavior of the promiscule or the nymphomaniac. It would hardly be good psychology to argue that some people behave in certain ways because they are *not* going to feel guilty about it. Not feeling guilty helps to pave the way for morally or socially unacceptable behavior, as we see so clearly exemplified in the psychopath; but that does not help us to understand the dynamics of the behavior itself. The violator of correct sexual codes is expressing in his behavior certain feelings and compulsions just as surely as the person who is dominated by the mask of hatred or by the lure of inferiority.

In Ruth's case, for example, she was driven by an uncontrollable desire to be with and make love to the "other man." This despite the fact that it was ruining her marriage, destroying her husband's love, wrecking her religious life, breaking up another family, and alienating all of her family and many of her friends. This is the price she was ready and even willing to pay for her private anarchy of feeling.

"I can't help myself," she told me in one of the early interviews. "I want to be with him no matter what the cost. I know that it's wrong, that it will wreck his marriage, that it is contrary to everything I have learned from my home and religion, and that many persons will be hurt by what I am doing. But I am willing to accept all of this just to be with him." As she said this, I was reminded of Jane Porter's trenchant remark, "When the cup of any sensual pleasure is drained to the bottom, there is always poison in the dregs."

This is sex without guilt in its most glaring form. It knows no conscience, it ignores all principles, and it violates every rule of acceptable conduct. Call it lust if you will, or nymphomania, or pathological self-indulgence. The important point is that we have here another striking incidence of the dethronement of reason by the anarchy of feeling.

Unfortunately, cases like these are not at all as rare as we would like to believe. The following incident would be almost amusing were it not for the tragic impact that it had on the lives of a number of people. I had been invited to talk to a large group of dedicated people who had banded together for the purpose of fostering wholesome family relationships. My talk was on the mental hygiene of the family, suggesting how the principles of mental hygiene can be used to promote healthy and productive family life. About a week later I received a call from a young wife and mother who said she was part of the group to whom I had talked and that she would like to discuss with me certain aspects of her own marriage. She was an attractive young matron in her late twenties and the mother of five children, ranging in age from one to eight years. Her husband was a moderately successful engineer who was devoted to his family, his work, and his religion.

Jane started out by saying how much she had enjoyed my remarks about wholesome family living, and then proceeded to tell me of her long-standing love affair with a man in the neighborhood who was himself the father of two children. She had met this man at a neighborhood party and from the very moment of meeting had become involved in a furious, fast-moving love affair. As is usually true in cases of this kind, Jane's commitment to her lover was total. The fact that she was actively engaged in a movement dedicated to more effective family living and more wholesome marriage relationships seemed not to disturb her at all. Nor was she disturbed by the impact of her love affair on her husband and children, nor by its effect on her family and friends who were caught in the backwash of her sordid relationships. There was no guilt, despite the fact that Jane had been raised in a strict religious environment, and was still an active Church member. There was only passion and intense desire—the anarchy of feeling.

"All I know is that I want him, and that I am miserable when I am away from him. I don't care about his family or mine. I just want to be with him, and to feel his arms around me. Only in this way can I be really happy."

It would be wrong to assume that this sort of impulse and behavior is characteristic of the "weaker" sex. In point of fact, it is highly probable that the lure of promiscuity is more potent in men than in women, or at least is found more often in men than in women. There are countless men who never tire in their endless search for additional conquests, and what statistical evidence we have indicates that many married men become involved in illicit relationships sometime or other during the course of their marital career. The pattern of behavior is much the same as with promiscuous and love-hungry women. Consciousness and reason seem to be dominated by the need for new relationships, for new contacts, and especially for new conquests. The presence of feeling is clearly discernible, but guilt is often absent. No price is too big, no risk too great in the effort to satisfy the insatiable longing for sex-love relationships.

Typical of this special instance of the anarchy of feeling is the case of a man whom we shall call Jonathan. At the time of referral, Jonathan was a married man, thirty-six years of age, with a family of three children. He was a respected member of the community and a professional person of considerable standing. He had been married for twelve years and was regarded by his family, his colleagues, and his friends as an exemplary husband and father.

Despite these outward signs of moral respectability, Jonathan suffered from a sickness that affects many men—"Don Juanism." While he wanted nothing more in life than to be a devoted husband and father, he nevertheless felt driven by an inner compulsion to seek outside relationships that would lead to sexual excitement and eventual gratification.

"I don't know what it is that comes over me, Doctor. But at times I feel such a powerful need to make love to someone other than my wife that I can't control it. After it is all over, and the relationship dissolved, I feel ashamed and disgusted with myself, but before long the same old pattern repeats itself. At times I get so depressed that I think of killing myself, but I am too much of a coward for that. Maybe that's what's wrong with me. Maybe I'm just a moral coward who can't control his own feelings and impulses."

"Does this behavior make you feel at all guilty?"

"No, it doesn't. And that's the funny thing about it. While I know that I am not acting in a way that society expects me to, and that I am degrading my relationships with my family, there is no real guilt associated with my conduct. I have sometimes likened myself in my own mind to an alcoholic who knows that he is destroying himself and his family but doesn't really care as long as he is able to satisfy his craving. That's the way it is with me. When this compulsion comes over me, all I can think about is satisfying the urge to find a love partner. I only feel ashamed because I know that I am not acting according to accepted standards. But I don't really feel guilty, because my need is so great that it is impossible to feel guilty about the behavior. All I know is that there is tremendous satisfaction in finding the right person, and guilt has nothing to do with it."

Here, again, we see how powerful feelings can become. However, whereas the story of guilt without sex will teach us how influential guilt can be, the story of sex without guilt shows us what contrary feelings can do. In the promiscuous person there is an insatiable longing for a kind of experience that many persons know nothing about. It is a vague and poorly defined longing that defies precise analysis. It is in part a longing for love and acceptance, unusual excitement, sexual experience, and other experiences that the unfortunate victim finds hard to describe. It has a lot to do with physical contact, but it is also related to such diverse phenomena as sexual identity, affection, loneliness, and other emotional needs.

Let us examine for a moment the motivations and characteristics of the typical Don Juan. What is it that drives him on from one conquest to another? What particular satisfactions does he get from these conquests? Is it that he considers himself to be so attractive and sexually powerful that he delights in achieving one conquest after another? Does he really believe that he is "God's gift to women," and therefore should distribute his gifts of love quite generously? It is extremely doubtful whether any one of these hypotheses is valid. The Don Juan we are talking about is quite unlike the gay Lothario of fiction who strikes fire in the heart of every young maiden or older matron who crosses his path. There may be in fact as in fiction such lovers whose destiny it is to erase the loneliness from the hearts of lonely women, but it is a doubtful hypothesis. It is much more probable that some men, single or married, are driven into the arms of different women in order to gratify deep, unconscious needs that have to do with such things as self-identity, masculinity, and inferiority. Certainly, we can be sure that much of this behavior has little intrinsic relationship to either love or sex.

The typical promiscule or Don Juan is a person who has deep, unconscious misgivings *about his own sex identity*. He worries a great deal about his manhood, and finds it difficult to identify the criteria of masculinity. Like every male, he wants very much to be a man, but there are many question marks in his psyche that indicate unanswered questions. "Am I really a man in the fullest sense of the term? Do I possess the priceless quality of masculinity? Am I feminine, or perhaps even homosexual? Can I function adequately as a male, especially in a sexual situation? What can I do to prove that I am a man?"

These are the questions that hammer away mercilessly at the uncertain identity of the Don Juan. In that area of identity where truth cannot be compromised to the slightest degree, he stands aghast at his own uncertainty. In a world that insists on sharp distinctions between male and female, he feels frightened and alone because he cannot be sure of what his position is. And yet the demands of sex identity are such that he must be sure. And it is this demand that forces him into behavior that will assure him of his masculinity and thus, he hopes, answer forever the question of his sex identity.

This is perhaps the primary motivation of the sexually promiscuous man or woman. The need to be a man, and the need to be a woman, are such fundamental and powerful elements in the dynamics of the human psyche that certainty will be purchased at any price. Moreover, there is a great deal of gratification that accrues to sexual conquest or illicit love relationships. When, therefore, gratification is added to the need for sexual identity the motivation becomes almost irresistible. This applies to women just as thoroughly as it applies to men whenever there is failure or confusion in the area of sexual identity.

However, it would be a mistake to assume that every person involved in promiscuous relationships was motivated by the need for sexual identity. There are other elements that must be taken into account if we are to understand this part of the anarchy of feeling. In quite a number of cases it reflects early emotional deprivation, that is, the absence of satisfying love relationships during childhood, and the unhappy victim figuratively roams the earth searching for the emotional gratifications that were denied him in his formative years. In still other instances it represents a constantly repeated effort to recapture the emotional gratifications of earlier relationships, particularly those with the father or mother. There is also the possibility that sexual relationships are used for self-degrading purposes or for degrading the partner involved.

How often in counseling we hear the statement that there is no real pleasure or gratification in the illicit behavior, but it does offer a means of gaining the upper hand where the opposite sex is concerned. Sex is often a powerful instrument for the control of human relationships.

As one client, a nineteen-year-old college girl, stated it, "I've never really gotten much out of sex relationships, and I doubt very much whether I have ever reached a climax. But when you're as unattractive as I am it's a good way of gaining attention and keeping some of the fellows in line. I suppose you would say it is wrong to use sex in this way, but I don't feel guilty about it. Sometimes a girl has no alternative if she is going to get a fellow at all. I often hate myself for it, and I know that it's wrong, but I haven't felt guilty about it for a long time."

In the tragic panorama of this young girl's life all of the forces of evil came together. Rejected by unloving parents, and unable to identify with her hypercritical mother, she presents the complete picture of the promiscuous female. She acts constantly to degrade herself and to degrade others; conscience has been dulled to the point where guilt has disappeared; motivation is always directed toward self-centered gratification, acceptance, and attention; and the anarchy of feeling has obliterated all moral sensibilities and self-control. Although keenly intelligent, at nineteen she has descended into a limbo of sexual corruption and excess that borders on the pathological. She delights in recounting her numerous affairs, and enjoys the pain her behavior brings to her parents and friends. Her sickly attachment to older men suggests a strong identification with her father and the typical unconscious, incestuous relationship that Freud referred to as the Electra complex. This is very probable in such cases. And yet the antipathy and rebellion toward the father is of such magnitude as to suggest a reaction against the identification. In other words, this unhappy young girl is expressing in her sexual behavior all of the confusion and resentment caused by unhappy relationships in childhood.

This story could be told over and over again, with new characters and new places, but it would not sound materially different. In every instance there is the tragic picture of broken relationships, promises and resolutions unkept, a conscience whose voice has been stilled by excessive indulgence, unhappy and distorted childhood experiences, and an endless panorama of sordid behavior and unwholesome relationships. It is a frightening picture of the dethronement of reason and human sensibility framed by the dominion of feeling. It is a kind of anarchy that is seldom out-pointed in strength or in violence by any of the other feelings that tend toward the destruction of the human mind. Small wonder that it so often successfully resists the intrusion of friendly advice, counseling, or even psychotherapy.

"All sensuality is one," said Thoreau, *"though it takes many forms, as all purity is one. It is the same whether men eat, or drink, or cohabit, or sleep sensually. They are but one appetite, and we only need to see a person do any of these things to know how great a sensualist he is."*

4 GUILT WITHOUT SEX

God hath yoked to guilt her pale tormentor, misery.

—BRYANT.

THERE WERE seven people in the group besides the therapist—
four men and three women. They looked like any other
group of relatively young people, ranging in age from twenty-
three to thirty-five, and one might suppose that they had come
together to discuss the next political campaign or how to
organize a church bazaar. For the most part, they were well-
dressed, good-looking young people who represented different
areas of the business or professional world. They sat in a half-
circle, more or less facing each other, and seemed to be waiting for a signal from the leader. They were, in other words,
seven human beings who had been coming together every
Tuesday night to participate in that strange and provocative
game called group psychotherapy.

For a while they just sat there staring at each other or looking down at the floor, and the therapist patiently waited for
what he knew would happen sooner or later—the rupturing
of intolerable silence by some member of the group whose
feelings demanded some kind of expression. They had been
together for some months now, and several members had
shown unmistakable signs of a breakdown in the anarchy of
feelings. They sat quietly, waiting for something to happen.

And then the break came. Like a torrent of water, words
suddenly gushed forth from the smallest and the most timid

of the group—Doreen. It was as though a barrier was suddenly washed away, and the words tumbled out in a voice crescendoed by the powerful impetus of frustration.

Doreen leaned slightly forward in her chair, her hands tightly interlocked. She was obviously upset. "I don't know, Doctor, I have been coming here for quite a while, and I don't think that this group therapy is doing me any good. Right from the beginning I have told all of you about my guilt feelings, how they torture me day in and day out, how they make me do all sorts of crazy, compulsive things. At first it helped me to talk about it, and to share my feelings with others in the group, especially Jane and Mary, who seemed to have experiences similar to mine. But now I don't know. I feel just as guilty as I ever did—sometimes I feel even more guilty talking about it in front of a group. I don't know whether I am going to come to any more sessions. I don't think this is going to help me any."

From across the room came another voice, this time from the girl known as Mary. She was obviously more composed than Doreen, but her ideas were much the same. "I am afraid I feel pretty much as Doreen does. I can't seem to get rid of these horrible guilt feelings. No matter how much I talk about them, or how much I listen to other people telling about their guilt feelings, I just can't shake them loose. I feel guilty all the time, and I know that it has a lot to do with my compulsive hand-washing, my sense of contamination, and the need for orderliness that drives me out of my mind. But I can't seem to get control of these feelings, and I am not at all sure that group therapy will help me do it."

Here and there, among other members of the group, there was a slight nod of assent. Jane's mouth opened as though she, too, were ready to comment, but the fear in her eyes betrayed the fact that she wasn't quite ready to share her feelings with the others. The group lapsed into temporary silence. There came to my mind the words of Sewell, "Fear is the tax that conscience pays to guilt."

Leaving aside the complex and unanswered question as to whether group psychotherapy actually works, the important feature of this brief dialogue between two tormented human beings and the group which they had joined is the community of guilt feelings. As we have already seen, there are quite a few feeling states in the total anarchy of feeling which torture and maim the human mind; but there are few as capable of insidious damage as is the feeling of guilt. According to the theologians, man is born in original sin, and thus to sinfulness and consequently the conviction of guilt. That this is so is attested in large measure by the repeated use of the Confessional, and by the admission of guilt, or the protest against it, among peoples of every generation and culture.

The feeling of guilt, like the emotion of anger, is the inevitable outcome of certain circumstances to which it is inseparably related. Just as frustration will inevitably give rise to irritation, annoyance, or anger, so wrongdoing, when clearly perceived by the doer, will inevitably lead to the conviction or the feeling of guilt. Just as anger is nature's signpost of frustration, and thus provides the organism with the dynamic resources necessary to reduce or obliterate the frustrating element, so guilt-feeling is the inner sign of wrongdoing, which provides the psychic impetus by which the individual begins to set his moral house in order, asks forgiveness, or undertakes to do penance in order that the guilt and the sin to which it is attached may be wiped away, and a start made toward a better and more perfect life.

This kind of guilt you will easily recognize as *normal* guilt.

In exactly the same way that it is quite normal to experience anger or fear under certain circumstances, and abnormal not to do so, so is it normal to experience guilt feelings whenever we do something that we know to be wrong, and abnormal not to feel guilty under these same conditions. We are all surprised and shocked when we read about a brutal killing concerning which the murderer has no remorse. This we find extremely difficult to understand, because we know that in the same circumstances we ourselves would feel terribly guilty. It is this state of affairs, this total lack of guilt or remorse, that stamps the psychopathic personality; and one of the main reasons why he is classified as a psychopath is his inability to experience normal feelings, such as fear or guilt.

When, therefore, we imply that guilt is a part, and a particularly dangerous one, of the anarchy of feeling, we are not attempting to undermine the bastions of morality. We are not, in other words, referring to normal guilt. A prudent and a wise Nature has cleverly designed the human mind so that between and among all of its intricate facets there is mutual interchange and support. The human person's need for morality—to be a decent, respectable, and law-abiding individual—is given strong support by basic needs and feelings within the personality. Without fear or anger, shame, remorse, or guilt, and without the basic needs for love, integrity, and self-acceptance, morality might well become a pale shadow within the personality with neither the force nor the substance to influence human behavior one way or another.

Certainly it can be argued that *objectively* there is a moral order and a moral law, and that *subjectively* there is a conscience to enforce the dictates of the moral order. But without the dynamic impulses provided by human needs and emotions, the human mind becomes a car without a carburetor, a mechanism without a dynamics, divested of the force that it needs to do the things that must be done. Let it be noted that this arrangement is not a commitment to the anarchy of feeling; rather, it is an organization by which the various "parts" of the human psyche are geared precisely to each other so that the totality operates as a smoothly running organism. And just as a carburetor is of little use without a driver, so the human organism with its needs, instincts, and feelings, requires intelligence and will to steer it on its proper course and toward its own destiny.

The importance of recognizing the efficacy of normal guilt in sustaining a person's moral life is underscored by recent parallel developments in the fields of psychiatry and theology. I do not wish to go too far afield in this matter, but we may profitably digress for a moment to note the growing rapprochement between these two important disciplines. This growth is especially noteworthy in view of the fact that a few short years ago there was a strong antagonism between them, marked by mutual suspicion and virulent criticism. But now, while the wedding is still only a future possibility, the courtship has been going on for a number of years, and the engagement is not far off. In fact, they have already built a "house," The Academy of Religion and Mental Health, with headquarters in New York City.

This important development is pertinent to our analysis of guilt because theology is obviously the custodian of morality, and psychiatry the arbiter of things in the psychic realm. The clash between the two disciplines was strikingly exemplified in the argument over the empirical validity of conscience as against the superego, and the efficacy of the Confessional as against the analytic couch. The theologian insisted that conscience is capable of judging the morality of behavior and thus is instrumental in helping the individual to avoid sin and guilt, or to take necessary steps to eliminate them. In place of conscience, the psychoanalysts substituted the superego which they often insist is equivalent to the older concept of conscience, but which has turned out to be a pale image of the conscience we all once knew. Similarly, in the matter of over-coming the effects of sinfulness, and the guilt associated with it, psychiatry de-emphasized the concept of sinfulness and put forward the notion that the individual is more mentally dis-turbed than sinful. For many, the couch should take the place of the Confessional. In these two somewhat oversimplified in-stances of the conflict between religion and psychiatry, we can get an idea of how important it is to understand the nature of guilt and the various forms that it assumes. For example, if guilt *is* regarded solely as an abnormal or pathological phe-nomenon, then the religionists and the theologians *must* revamp their entire concept of morality. If, on the other hand, there is such a thing as normal guilt, the psychiatrist has to modify the position that all guilt is pathological. It is in such areas as this that the two disciplines have achieved mutual understanding, and are working much more closely together in a joint effort to alleviate human suffering.

The feelings of guilt that emerge so dramatically and con-sistently in the practice of counseling or psychotherapy are clearly part and parcel of the anarchy of feeling. Quite unlike the person who feels guilty after committing adultery, mastur-bation, or other behavior traditionally regarded as sinful, the patient with a morbid sense of guilt finds himself bound to the Procrustean bed of immorality without being able to tell exactly what the "immorality" is all about. If, for the sake of discussion, we use sexual immorality as a focal point, we have a clear-cut instance of *guilt without sex*. In such cases the hapless victim feels guilty all the time, but finds that he has to invent things about which he is supposed to feel guilty. This feeling, of course, is the bedrock of *scrupulosity*, one of the most damaging neurotic processes ever imposed on the mind of man.

As a case in point, let us look briefly at the unhappy life story of a young married woman whom we will call Joanne. Joanne is an attractive, blonde young woman of Germanic descent. She is only twenty-nine years of age, has been married four years, and is the mother of two children. By and large, she is happily married, particularly because her husband is a thoughtful, compassionate man who tries to understand his wife's problem, and who is quite willing to see that she gets the help she needs. Joanne complains very little about her husband, but she does find that married life is extremely difficult for her, especially where her sexual obligations and her role as a mother to the children are concerned. She feels, however, that if she could resolve her emotional problem, her attitude toward these demands would change, and her other problems would largely disappear.

The emotional problem to which Joanne refers revolves around a persistent, gnawing, senseless feeling of guilt. This feeling, Joanne explains, goes all the way back to early adolescence and seems to be associated with pubertal development and the first stirrings of sexual impulse and feeling. Characteristically, Joanne, like so many persons involved in the tyranny of guilt feelings, became extremely scrupulous during her early adolescent years, and remains so at the present time. Every little act, every personal imperfection, everything remotely tainted with sin or the possibility of sin, is grist for the inexorable mill of feeling that grinds constantly within her mind. If she disciplines the children too severely, if she does not discipline them severely enough, if she fails to perform her wifely duties, if she does not cooperate sexually with her husband, if she does not telephone her mother frequently, if her thoughts turn to sexual matters, and so on *ad infinitum*, she experiences pangs of guilt. Guilt is always with her, and spreads its poisonous tentacles to every phase of her life. Her thoughts are constantly tainted by the feeling that she is guilty of wrongdoing, no matter how perfectly correct her behavior has been.

As we might expect in a person who is devoutly Catholic, this deep and unassailable conviction of guiltiness affects not only her behavior, but her relationships with other people, and her religious aspirations as well. As with all Catholic patients suffering from guilt and scrupulosity, the religious practice of Confession—the one hope for release from the stranglehold of her guilt feelings—is fraught with uncertainty, anxiety, and unbearable self-reproach. Confession, which should be a source of peace and strength to the guilty sinner, becomes an excruciating ordeal. Typically, it is put off as long as possible, and then when the anguished victim of scrupulosity finally manages to force herself into the Confessional box, her Confession degenerates into a ritual of self-accusation, and the relating of thoughts and actions that by no stretch of the imagination could be called sinful. This is the typical story of Joanne, and of all of the other unhappy people who, because of some unfortunate twist in their early lives, become the tortured victims of guilt and scrupulosity.

It is interesting to note at this point that morbid or neurotic guilt affects morality and religion in a manner exactly contrary to that of normal guilt. As we explained before, normal guilt is the servant of morality and acts at the same time to bulwark the person's religious motives and ideals. This is its essential purpose, just as it is the purpose of fear to safeguard the individual from dangerous and threatening events. But abnormal and neurotic guilt does just the opposite; it weakens the moral fiber and robs the victim of any self-determination based upon the acceptance of principles and ideals. The primary motive in the scrupulous person is the fear of feeling guilty. The goodness or badness of behavior, or adherence to a moral code, have little to do with his conduct. He generally is a person free of moral taint, but only because of his deep sense of guilt, and not because of high moral standards.

Similarly, neurotic guilt and scrupulosity act to undermine not only religious practices, such as Confession, but also basic religious beliefs and commitments. God Himself is often the focal point of attack, because it is God who is responsible for the misery he is experiencing. Let Joanne tell you about this.

"You know, Doctor, I think I am losing my religion. I have always been what is considered a devout Catholic; I go to Mass regularly every Sunday, and I receive the Sacraments as often as I can. But sometimes I think it's all a sham; that I don't really believe all of the things that my religion has taught me, or even that God exists. You know how much trouble I have going to Confession, and more often than not I have just as much difficulty in receiving Communion, because I am sure that I have made a bad Confession. In this way I pile sacrilege on top of sacrilege." Joanne paused for a while as though she weren't sure that she wanted to continue with what she had in mind. I waited for her to go on. "Actually, Doctor, I am very angry with God. I feel terrible saying this, but it's the truth. I sometimes feel that if I could just get rid of religion and the idea of God, I could finally get rid of this terrible guilt feeling. After all, if it weren't for God and all of His rules, commandments, and threats, I wouldn't have to feel so guilty and afraid."

This is the common attitude and complaint of the guilt-ridden, scrupulous neurotic. The young lady, Betty, whom we shall meet in our analysis of hatred, expresses it a little differently, even though the basic idea is the same. As she puts it, "You know, Doctor, I don't think that my religion does me any good. I'm so angry with God all the time that it's a farce for me to go to church, or to receive the sacraments. And this makes me feel even more guilty. No matter what you say, I just can't believe that God is not responsible for my miserable, unhappy life. He could stop it any time that He wants to. It's His fault that I'm so lonely and unhappy all the time; and that bothers me a great deal because all I have to look forward to is the next life, and I don't suppose I will merit even that, the way I feel toward God. He never answers my prayers in this life, so I don't see why I can expect salvation in the next. I even feel guilty saying all this to you."

You can see from these few, brief excerpts how pervasive, neurotic guilt can eat its way into the moral and religious fiber of its victim until there is nothing left but the pale shadow of what was once a deeply religious person. Even the concept of God does not remain inviolate. But the ravaging process initiated by guilt does not stop at the moral and religious elements in the personality. It reaches also into the intellect. The scrupulous and guilt-ridden person—or, as Freud would have put it, the person with an overdeveloped superego—is by definition one who cannot distinguish between right and wrong, good and bad. His conscience is either underdeveloped or has deteriorated; and conscience, by definition, *is* the intellect directed toward the morality of acts.

Thus scrupulosity and guilt like poisonous amoebae infect

the whole personality until the disorder reaches the intellect itself. As one anguished college student expressed it: "I'm all confused. I don't know what to think anymore. I've gotten to the point where I can't act at all. If I do what is right and good, this will bring pleasure, and it is wrong to enjoy pleasure. If I do what is wrong, that is obviously intolerable, since I already feel so guilty. Therefore, I can't act at all." Significantly, he added shortly afterwards: "If I could just get rid of my belief in God, I wouldn't have all this difficulty. I've just about come to the decision that I'm going to abandon the God of my religion, and invent one of my own. Maybe then I could get rid of this awful guilt."

This intrusion of guilt into intellectual functioning, by which the power of selective judgment and discrimination is reduced to an ineffective ritual that transforms everything experienced into evil, is also carried forward into the area of self-determination. Typically, the victim of pathological guilt feelings finds it as impossible to control his feelings and his behavior as to make adequate discriminations. With monotonous repetition, he says again and again: "I can't help myself. I feel guilty, and there's nothing that I can do about it. I know that it is silly to think that everything that I do is wrong, but I can't help it. My feelings won't let me think anything else. I know that, from an objective standpoint, what I often think is wrong is not wrong. But my feelings tell me differently; and they are stronger than my intellectual judgment."

Here we see, in the simplest kind of language, how the anarchy of feeling establishes a stranglehold over the personality of its victim. We see how the will, or the power of self-control, has waned into ineffectuality. We see clearly what happens when the feelings gain dominion over the intellect, and then we know that in its wake will come rigidity, compulsiveness, and the breakdown of self-control. This happens with invariable consistency because the power of decision (and thus of self-control) is inherently dependent upon the power of discrimination. If we cannot make adequate judgments or discriminations, then we cannot be effective in making decisions. The one always hinges upon the other. And thus the corrosive influence of guilt creeps into the very citadel of human freedom. The anarchy of feeling, with guilt as its instrument, can achieve complete domain over the soul. No man can remain free unless he maintains executive control over his behavior; and, even more to the point, no man can be free who is the victim of his own feelings. Feelings, once they get out of hand, quickly make a mockery of man's only weapons of freedom, his intellect and his will.

The feeling of guilt and the obsession of scrupulosity are clearly reflected in the rigid and compulsive behavior that characterizes persons in whom they develop. Because the victim feels guilty, and therefore bad and dirty, there is likely to be an overwhelming sense of contamination, which the Freudians trace back (correctly) to the anal period of development. This feeling of being contaminated invariably leads to ritualistic behavior so clearly exemplified in the hand-washing compulsion. It is as though the victim of guilt, like Shakespeare's Lady Macbeth, must somehow cleanse himself of the guilt that is his constant companion. Thus we are not surprised when he tells us that he feels the compulsion to wash his hands many times a day, sometimes as often as forty or fifty times.

But the rigidity and the compulsiveness do not end with this simple ritual. The bathroom basin must be scrubbed again and again until it is absolutely free of any possible contamination. The faucets must be scrupulously checked to see that no single drop of water escapes from them. Clothes must be arranged in meticulous order, as must the various articles on the desk. In every department of daily living, there must be cleanliness and order, order and cleanliness, until the rigid ritualizing takes over completely and freedom disappears.

It is obvious from this description that compulsive cleanliness and orderliness go hand in hand, and for a very good reason. Both symptoms express with striking clarity the type of personality and psychic structure involved in guilt feelings and scrupulosity. Obsessive cleanliness reflects the feeling of guilt that constantly plagues the individual, whereas the compulsive orderliness reflects the *disorder* in the mind of the patient. In much the same way that the unfortunate victim tries to wash away the guilt by being scrupulously clean, he hopes to bring order into his life by creating order in the objective world. In its own way, each symptom helps to protect the sufferer from the conflicts and inadequacies within his own personality. If it is true that "Order is Heaven's first law," and "Cleanliness is next to Godliness," the compulsive neurotic can certainly argue that he is on the side of the angels. In this we see part of the logic of symptom-formation. Symptoms are forms of behavior that develop to protect the individual from his own faults.

This same line of reasoning explains why the victim of guilt and scrupulosity will invariably tend in the direction of *perfectionism*. This trend is already suggested in the symptoms of cleanliness and orderliness. Here again the symptomatic argument is very simple: "If I do everything perfectly, if I tolerate no mistakes or faults in whatever I do, then there can be no imperfection in me." Note how similar this attitude is to compulsive orderliness, since orderliness is an aspect of perfection. I am reminded here of the students who can never get their term papers in on time because they must be revised again and again in order to eliminate all flaws and imperfections.

Let us observe that perfectionism is not long reserved for the person himself; it soon begins to spread to other persons and situations within the environment. I remember one student who sat down and wrote out with meticulous precision the characteristics of the girl whom he expected to marry as soon as he could find her. There were about thirty qualities involved, and when put together they represented a composite of Joan of Arc, the Blessed Virgin, Mary Magdalen, Catherine the Great, and Marilyn Monroe. This device worked very nicely for him since his guilt and scrupulosity typically revolved around sex, and thus his perfectionism protected him from ever becoming involved seriously with girls. When perfectionism is projected to other persons, it begins to interfere seriously with interpersonal relationships, and still further complicates the problems of the unhappy victim of guilt. Here again we see how the anarchy of feeling spreads its insidious influence to all aspects of the victim's life.

We have been speaking rather generally of two basic forms of guilt—normal as opposed to abnormal, pathological, or neurotic, guilt. Before we proceed further with our analysis, let us stop for a moment and look more closely at the latter form. This will enable us to define more precisely what abnormal guilt really is, and where it comes from. In this category belongs first the generalized, pervasive sense of guilt— the "I always feel guilty" attitude—that we have concentrated on so far. This feeling is conscious, but it is vague and ill-defined, and leaves the person with an itchy sense of uneasiness and wrongdoing that plagues every waking moment. There is also another form of guilt about which we have said very little, although it is not basically different from the first kind.

This guilt is real, but it is out of all proportion to the act from which it springs. A patient complains that he has committed the unpardonable sin, when actually he has only been a bad boy. Or every little act of wrongdoing, every venial digression from the strictest norm of morality, is regarded as mortally sinful.

Thus a client of mine would tell me about her employer, how sometimes he reneged on overtime pay, or how he would flirt with her occasionally, or how he spoke disparagingly of his wife. Then suddenly she would stop short and ask herself, "What am I saying? I shouldn't be telling you these things about him. Now I have done something wrong again. I have destroyed his good name." This sort of reaction is very likely to happen in counseling and psychotherapy, especially if such a client gets into the area of sexual difficulties. These people cannot make a distinction between sex talk and talk *about* sex. To them, everything sexual is sinful, and therefore to talk about sexual problems is also sinful. In these instances we have a clear example of guilt without sex.

There are times also when guilt is buried deep within the unconscious and thus affects feelings and behavior only indirectly. However, unconscious guilt is something to be reckoned with, since it can cause a great deal of psychic harm. This form of guilt is the result of *repression*, which means that the person involved finds it impossible to tolerate the guilt at a conscious level. This fact itself is indicative of the potential distortion that unconscious guilt can bring about. We see this type of guilt manifested quite often in the extremely moralistic person who stands ready to condemn all forms of human weakness, as well as the people in whom these weaknesses are found; we see it in the behavior of reformers and do-gooders who must change the world, and the

people in it, to conform to their own moralistic excesses. We
see it also in the compulsive tendency to find fault with others,
to criticize, to punish, and, in general, to function as the right
hand of God in meting out justice.

Lynch mobs and vigilante groups are good examples of
"justice" determined by unconscious guilt, in which case guilt
and hostility blend together in determining behavior. The
psychological value of such behavior is quite obvious. The
reasoning goes like this: "If I can project my guilt on to others
and blame them, I will get rid of my own guilt. This will work
especially well if I can punish them for their 'wrongdoing.' "
You understand, of course, that none of this projection, blaming, or punishment is done with the knowledge that unconscious guilt is at work. It all takes place without one's perceiv-
ing the relationship between guilt and his own behavior, and
this unawareness enables him to maintain the fiction that he
has been a very noble and just person. In instances like these,
then, the cause of the behavior or of the symptoms is the repressed guilt, and we may safely assume that this guilt was
repressed because the original experience which aroused guilt
was so unpleasant or so frightening as to be intolerable at the
conscious level.

But the situation is somewhat different when we consider
the other two forms of guilt previously described. In the case
of guilt that is wholly out of proportion to the act, or in cases
where guilt is a generalized, persistent feeling that pervades
psychic life, the guilt reflects other factors in the personality.
When we listen to such persons' tales of woe, about how
many sins they have committed, how guilty they feel, we get
the definite impression that deep within themselves, at the very
core of their being, they stand convicted of being no good, of
being bad or evil, of being worthless. Such clients will often

say quite directly: "I feel as though I am basically bad, that I am no good. I must have been a very bad or obnoxious child whom no one could stand to have around him. I must have been bad, and that's why I feel so guilty now."

In this condensation of many statements from numerous clients, we begin to see what lies beneath the pervasive feeling of guilt manifested so starkly in the scrupulous person. They are trying to tell us that when they were small, they were bad and therefore unwanted, not only by unimportant people in the environment, but by the most important people in their lives—their parents. They are saying to us that they were rejected, that they did not belong to anyone, that they were never really loved; and therefore they must have been very bad or very evil. This is the only explanation that they can find for such total rejection. The guilt that they feel, therefore, is unlike normal guilt insofar as the guilt does not stem from illicit, immoral, or bad behavior. The victim reasons that he must have been bad because he feels so guilty; but the badness from which the guilt springs is the result of rejection or the withholding of love rather than of bad behavior. How poignantly one client expressed it when she said: "I must have been an obnoxious child." We must always remember that to the young child the morality of later life has very little meaning. For him to be bad it is not necessary to lie, to steal, to blaspheme, or to be disobedient. All that is necessary is for him to be unwanted or rejected, and then he will feel bad the rest of his life. And he will also feel guilty. This is the essential key to an understanding of neurotic guilt, especially since it has nothing to do with immorality.

When a child is deeply frustrated in respect to basic needs, he will not only feel rejected and unwanted and bad; he will also become deeply angry. As we shall see more fully in our analysis of hostility (Chapter 5), frustration almost always generates anger, and anger quickly develops into hostility. Thus the child made to feel bad by the parent's attitude of rejection will soon pile hostility on top of the negative feeling germinating in the personality. The guilt already present will thus be compounded by the added guilt he feels for being angry with his parents.

You will remember the young lady, Joanne, whom we introduced at the beginning of this discussion. Joanne's guilt problem is one of the clearest instances I have seen in which pervasive guilt, hostility, and scrupulosity blended into a psychic pattern that poisoned every moment of her waking life. As far back as she could remember, Joanne never got along with her mother, who clearly and unmistakably favored an older sister. Joanne was aware of this from the time that she was five years old, and the hatred of her mother grew to such proportions that there was almost a constant and open warfare between them. Already burdened by the guilt that resulted from her mother's rejection, her remaining strength was almost crushed by the additional guilt resulting from her hostility. Even though she is now married, the conflict rages on.

"I don't know what I am going to do with my feelings toward my mother. Even after all these years, I still feel so hostile toward her that I shudder whenever the phone rings for fear she is calling me. I find it almost impossible to invite her for dinner, because I just can't stand being around her. I know that this is wrong, and that I shouldn't feel this way, and as a result I feel even more guilty than I did before. Sometimes I feel so bad and so guilty I can't stand it. And to make matters worse, I can't even go to Confession because that is more painful than the guilt itself."

From this analysis of abnormal guilt we see why the person

loses the faculty for discrimination and decision, and why the guilt spreads to so many different acts regardless of whether they are moral or not. As distinct from normal guilt which always *follows* unacceptable or immoral behavior, neurotic guilt always *precedes* behavior. In other words, guilt exists long before the act to which it *supposedly* refers. Neurotic guilt reaches out for and engulfs behavior irrespective of its moral quality. The nature of guilt is such that, to the disordered mind of the neurotic, a perverted logic requires antecedent immoral behavior. "I *feel* guilty, therefore I must *be* guilty. To *be* guilty I must have done something wrong. Therefore, I have done something wrong." Thus, in a desperate effort to make some sense of his guilt feelings, the unhappy victim searches for anything that will fit into the pattern of his guilt.

As one such person said to me, "I feel very guilty because I asked my father to carry my suitcases up three flights of stairs. In that way I risked causing him a heart attack, which is very thoughtless and cruel of me." In her mind, to be thoughtless and cruel is to commit a wrong, and therefore she could justify her guilt. The fact that her father is a hale and hearty man, and suffered not one whit from the task imposed upon him, did not enter into the logic of her evaluation. It is this tendency of existing, antecedent guilt to reach out, as it were, and engulf behavior that helps us to understand why scrupulosity can reach the bizarre proportions that it does. The thoroughly scrupulous person can find guilt in almost any type of action or relationship.

Because sexual feelings, behavior, and relationships are loaded with possibilities for "wrongdoing," it is quite natural that a great deal of guilt feelings and of scrupulosity should focalize on them. In the case of normal guilt it is to be expected that much of it will be derived from sex behavior; but where neurotic guilt is concerned, we again see that guilt precedes the behavior or the relationship, and thus the phrase "guilt without sex." For example, one such scrupulous person felt very guilty because of an attraction to her employer. This she felt guilty about because of its sexual implications, and also because of the fact that the man was married. However, when the so-called attraction was analyzed, it was found to be entirely devoid of any sexual element, and amounted to nothing more than the fact that she found him interesting and likable. This tendency to "sexualize" behavior or relationships is a direct outgrowth of guilt feelings, and of the fear of sex that is aroused by its direct relation to guilt feelings. In most instances in which guilt is anchored to pseudo-sexual problems, it will be found that there is actually very little sexuality in the life of the person. The fact is that sexuality threatens to arouse so much guilt that the client is completely protected against any sexual outbreak.

It need hardly be pointed out that these abnormal and neurotic guilt feelings have their analogues in the experiences of countless normal people. Guilt, whether normal or abnormal, is a universal phenomenon, and a problem that everyone must confront squarely and courageously. The difficulty with guilt is that it must in some way or other be expiated, and this is the basic reason why Freud referred to it as "the need for punishment." There is a great deal of truth in this idea because certainly we do not feel right until the guilt in us has been expiated in one way or another, usually through some form of reparation, punishment, or penance. Because the person with neurotic guilt finds it impossible to expiate his feelings of guilt, no matter how many times he tries to do so through the medium of Confession or contrition, he finds it very difficult to live with his guilt. Also, because the guilt is not tied to immoral behavior, or reprehensible conduct, but rather to the conviction that he is bad or worthless, the hapless victim finds little solace in the ordinary means of reducing guilt feelings, and thus turns toward counseling or psychotherapy. Certainly, since his problem is essentially psychological rather than moral, his hope for a reduction of guilt is most likely to be realized through a psychological approach. His problem is deep and pervasive, but skillful psychotherapy can often help him to destroy this anarchy of feeling and restore the primacy of intellect and will.

5 THE MASK OF HATRED

Hatred is the madness of the heart.

—BYRON.

THE YOUNG MAN sitting across from me was barely twenty years old, a sophomore in college. He was a nice-looking youngster, somewhat slight of build, with a pleasant face and a healthy crop of wavy, black hair. At the moment he was somewhat fidgety because we had gotten into some material that was very disturbing to him. I had asked him how he felt about his parents, who seemed to form an important backdrop to his problem. As we talked, and the floodgates of feeling opened wide in the process called "ventilation," his young and handsome face became almost livid and changed into a mask of muscular contortions that only extreme anger, hostility, and unbridled hate can produce. The nice young man, in the course of a few moments, had become a raging furnace of emotions. The mask of hatred had descended over him, and it became very difficult to recognize that this was the same nice young man who had entered my office only a few minutes before.

He was telling me about his parents. "I loathe and despise them. My mother and father are the most despicable bastards that I ever expect to meet. They've never done anything for me that was any good, and ever since I can remember, they have used me and exploited me just for their own selfish purposes. Take my mother, for example. All she ever wanted out of me was a chance to boast that her son was in the Priesthood. She didn't give a goddamn about me—all she thought of was herself. And my father—he's so damned passive and weak that he didn't have the guts to stand up to her and stop her from doing this to me. Boy, the happiest day of my life was when I came out of that seminary and I let her know that she wasn't going to exploit me any longer."

I waited for the right opening and said, "Bill, all of that was some time ago. Don't you think it's about time that you got rid of some of these feelings of hostility, and began to realize that even parents make mistakes, parents who often love their children very deeply?"

This did not placate Bill in the least. In fact, some of his hostility began to turn in my direction—a not unexpected result. He went on for another twenty or twenty-five minutes, excoriating his parents, glorying in his hatred, and repeatedly emphasizing that no one is any damn good and no one can be trusted, especially those who are supposed to love you, because they're sure to let you down.

Here we have a typical and glaring instance of the mask of hatred; if ever the anarchy of feeling is revealed in all its naked horror, this is the time. The young boy we have called Bill was completely dominated and completely immobilized by his feelings of hostility and hatred. For him there was no control, no possibility of a change in the direction of more positive, healthier emotions. Bill's feelings toward his parents, and toward people in general, constituted an absolute anarchy that allowed no freedom of expression. Although a bright boy, and an outstanding student in his class, in the area of human relationships his intellect was completely dethroned and could play no part whatever in helping him to move toward other people.

So dominated by the feeling of hostility was he that when he became interested in a lovely young girl at a place of business where he worked part time, he quit his job rather than allow himself to become involved with her in any kind of positive relationship. "What right has she got to interfere with my feelings of hatred? I would like to love her, yes. But if I let myself fall in love with her, I would have to give up my hostility toward my parents and toward everyone else; and this I refuse to do. My hatred is the only protection that I have against getting involved with people; and I don't want to get involved with them. They're no damned good. No one has ever done anything for me, and what's more, I'm not going to let anybody get even close to me. That's why I quit my job."

What a tragedy that a young man should enter the vestibule of adult, responsible living charged with such feelings that will limit his achievements, his self-realization, and his relationships with other people. Yet he is only one of countless thousands who wear the mask of hostility—countless thousands who, living in an anarchy of feeling, find life disagreeable, friendships lagging and falling apart because of the repeated thrusts of hostility, themselves tortured by their inability to get along with others, and often feeling intolerably guilty because those whom they should love are the direct targets for their hostility.

I am reminded of a young couple who have gone together for a long, long time. She is a strikingly beautiful girl of Eastern European descent, a college graduate who was once chosen Queen of the Campus. The young man is a teacher of history with a Master's degree from a prominent university. Both are unusually intelligent, skilled in the arts of expression and communication, and possessed of the easy grace and charm that come with breeding and education. They are such a nice couple—until they are alone together. And then in a few moments, maybe a half-hour, a flame burning deep within the unconscious of each one, sets afire the unrequited passions of their childhood. Before long they are two raging victims of hostility, calling each other unmentionable names, hurling invectives, throwing objects, and spitting and cursing at each other until the fire is burned out for lack of fuel, or one of them is carted off to the hospital to have sixteen stitches taken where a heavy fist rammed in hateful fury against a beautiful eye. This is the unadorned, naked picture of hostility and hatred. This is the anarchy of feeling run amuck. This is the picture of two intelligent, educated human beings tearing at each other like primitive beasts of prey because in them feelings are king, and the intellect their pawn.

To the average person, the hostile, aggressive, and enraged human being, blinded and almost stupefied by the feelings that sweep over and engulf his conscious powers, is a strange and somewhat frightening character. This is true of many other instances in which feeling dominates behavior, but it is perhaps most strikingly exemplified in the expressions of rage and hatred.

And yet, despite the strangeness of such behavior, we are daily witnesses to numerous instances of rage and hatred. On the international scene, there are the Nazi ovens of destruction, the concentration camps, the enforced starvation of hated enemies, the unbelievable brutality of war, and the wholesale destruction of innocent men, women, and children throughout the world. In these horrible examples of man's inhumanity to man, we see human hatred and rage unleashed in all of its terrible intensity. There is no fury in the brute animal that can match the destructive rage of *homo sapiens*, when rage is aided and abetted by the scheming, cunning intellect of man. Here, in these acts of sadistic fury and hatred, we see in bright colors how the feelings and emotions of man not only gain tyrannical control but actually enlist the support of man's higher faculties. No single specimen in the kingdom of the brute ever possessed the imagination or the intelligence required to bring into reality the destructiveness of the atomic bomb, germ warfare, or the concentration camps.

These are more striking instances of hostility run amuck, but it is not at all difficult to find similar examples on the local scene. The muggings, the beatings, the attacks of rape, the merciless stompings, the pistol-whipping, and all the other murderous paraphernalia of the youthful gang member and the hardened criminal are just so many additional instances of human rage and hostility. While the big city abounds in this type of behavior, there is no community entirely free of hatred and fury. In one community we witness the stark terror of a lynch mob; in another the bombing of an innocent victim of racial intolerance; and in still another the vicious bludgeoning of a defenseless old man. In every one of these instances of senseless maiming and destruction of life, rage and hatred are clearly the motivating forces. And we see again how the anarchy of feeling can lead men and women down the path of ruthless destruction and insensate behavior.

If you want to understand such behavior, senseless as it is, it is important to realize that it is only the last link in a chain of responses that begins with such relatively innocuous things as teasing, sarcasm, excessive criticism, and domineering. We have drawn a simple diagram to show how all of these responses can be arranged on a continuum from one extreme to the other. Such an arrangement makes it easier for us to grasp the essential fact that underneath all of the hostility, the hatred, and the fury that at times possesses the human mind, there is a single emotional undercurrent of *anger*. Significantly, anger, like love and fear, is one of the most basic and the most primitive of human emotions; and it is these emotions that are most likely to establish an anarchy of feeling in the human person.

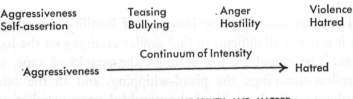

Aggressiveness	Teasing	. Anger	Violence
Self-assertion	Bullying	Hostility	Hatred

Continuum of Intensity

Aggressiveness ⟶ Hatred

CONTINUUM OF ANGER, HOSTILITY AND HATRED

Freud had suggested the interesting theory that all of this rage, hostility, and destructiveness came from an impulse or drive in the human mind to which he gave the term *aggression*. While at first he tended to overemphasize the instinct of sex, to the exclusion of other motivations, Freud later came to the position that some human behavior required the assumption of another basic drive which is just as fundamental in the development of personality as sex; and this drive is aggression. And certainly there is considerable evidence, in daily life as in the clinic, of aggression in the behavior of human beings. In fact, a great deal of the *aggressiveness* so clearly exemplified in the typical American business man is nothing more than aggression channelled into a mode of behavior that has been made socially acceptable. This neat little trick is accomplished by the simple expedient of emphasizing the importance of competition and of "getting ahead." Actually, of course, it is just as distasteful to most people as is the naked aggression of the child who bites his playmate in the leg; but it does serve something of a useful purpose insofar as it enables the ambitious business man to work off some of his hostilities without doing too much damage in the process.

However, while the concept of aggression is useful, and fits neatly into the continuum of hostile responses, it is not necessary to go along with the idea that it represents a basic impulse or drive in the human personality. I am not going to get embroiled here in the niceties of psychological theory, but I merely want to indicate that we can understand hostility and hatred a lot easier by referring it back to its primary source, which is the emotion of anger. This everyone understands, because everyone experiences anger at one time or another, whereas he may be a stranger to aggression. We can well imagine that the shy, timid, mild-mannered milk-toast type of person is not going to take too readily to the idea that everyone is endowed by nature with powerful aggressive tendencies.

It is the failure of such theories to encompass all instances of human behavior, or all varieties of human character, that makes them suspect. Certainly, there is a great deal of aggression at loose in the world, a pattern so clearly exemplified in the Soviet Union's approach to any type of problem. But to go from a common type of behavior to a universal proposition regarding the nature of man is an extremely doubtful procedure. We know for sure that all men are capable of becoming angry, and will do so at one point or another in their lives; but we cannot say with equal certainty that all men are inherently aggressive. Therefore we must try to find a better explanation for the mask of hatred than the theory of aggression.

There is a very simple formula that we can use to explain how the mask of hostility develops in any single individual. Let us return for a moment to the continuum of responses that we diagrammed a few pages back. I said there that at the opposite extreme of hatred and fury are such ordinary phenomena of behavior as teasing, sarcasm, and excessive criticism. Now what is it that causes a young boy to tease his sister to the point of exasperation, or a wife to nag (that is, to criticize) her husband from morning until night? If you will look at the simple diagram below, you will see quickly enough what happens in situations like this. In *every* such instance there are two common elements: (1) a need (motive, desire, or goal); and (2) frustration. Quite understandably then, as the diagram indicates, whenever the need, motive, desire, or

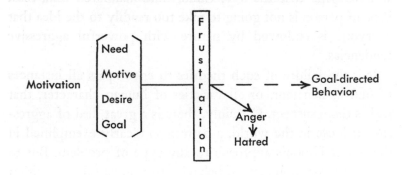

THE ORIGINS OF HOSTILITY AND HATRED

goal is frustrated (blocked), anger is an inevitable by-product. Take away a child's toy, break off an engagement, fire an employee, call someone an insulting name, block traffic, or do any one of a thousand things that stifle a need or its expression, and you will witness the quick flame of anger. The relationships diagrammed above will, in such instances, leave the dead pages of description and become a living, pulsating experience in which motivating forces, frustration, and anger become the threads from which the mask of hatred is woven.

It is anger, then, growing out of repeated or chronic frustration, that constitutes the core of hostility and hatred, and that in its extreme form is expressed in insensate rage and fury. The key which unlocks the secret of chronic and continuous hostility is the relationship between frustration and the drive that is blocked. If the drive (need, motive) does not possess a great deal of significance for the person, then the fact that it is blocked will have relatively little meaning. For example, we would not expect hostility to develop in a youngster on being denied admission into college when he didn't want to go in the first place. He may have wanted to make his parents happy (motive), and thus applied for admission, but he is able to shrug it off without any difficulty when the motive is blocked. Conversely, we would expect a great deal of hostility to develop if a person is frustrated in his ambition to succeed in his job and thus acquire the status and recognition that are so important to him. It isn't long before the anger and hostility become quite apparent in such situations.

If now we switch our psychic camera and focus on needs and drives that are even more significant than status and recognition, it becomes crystal clear why in some instances hostility reaches enormous proportions. If we go back to the case of Bill, who hated his parents with such passionate intensity, we will see that the basic reason is the frustration of his need for love and acceptance. And the longer and more continuous the frustration, the more chronic will the hostility become. The need for love (acceptance, belonging, being wanted) is such a basic demand of the human personality that its chronic frustration can lead to the most serious personality disorders, including schizophrenia. If we review Bill's complaint against his parents, we will see that he felt deeply rejected, and it was this rejection that acted as the well-spring of hostility and hatred. As I have indicated in the simple diagram below, rejection causes severe frustration of the need for love, which causes psychic pain and anger, and this situation in turn generates hostility or hatred.

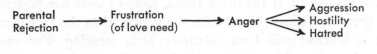

RELATIONS BETWEEN LOVE, REJECTION, AND HOSTILITY

What is clear from this analysis is that hostility and hatred are nurtured only in a special kind of emotional soil. There are many children in whom parents provoke anger, just as there are many employees who are at times angered by their superiors. But there are relatively few children (or employees) who become the victims of chronic hostility or hatred. Much the same is true of chronic anxiety, which we will take up later on. While everyone experiences anxiety at one time or another, the majority of people do not become anxiety neurotics. Other ingredients must be added to the soil before it nurtures chronic hostility or anxiety.

In the case of rejection, and similar conditions that involve deep-seated frustration, the added ingredients typically include such elements as fear, degradation, and severe ego-damage. When a child is rejected by parents who are unloving, jealous, or given to playing favorites, he not only feels unloved, but he becomes afraid and lonely, and develops a deep sense of worthlessness, of not being wanted or accepted. His reasoning is very simple: "If my own parents don't love me or want me, I can't be worth much. I must be very bad, or I must have done something very bad to make them stop loving me." Once this state of mind is reached, the whole complex is liable to further development in the direction of deep-seated guilt. It is these reactions that cause ego-damage, that is, an injury to the inner core of the personality from which recovery is almost impossible. When these things happen, the human mind becomes fertile soil for the growth of hostility and hatred. The same thing happens in other situations when a person is made to feel small or worthless, when he is downgraded—in other words, when there is severe ego-damage. If to all of this is added the element of fear, hostility is an inevitable outcome.

The relation between fear and hostility is clearly exemplified in situations where rejection, degradation, or ego-damage are not so readily apparent. For example, in the Nazi atrocities against the Jewish people, and in our own racial and religious bigotries here in America, we see intense and destructive hatred sprouting in a different climate and in a different soil than we described previously. In these instances fear is an essential ingredient. The typical Southerner, whose hatred breaks out in tirades against desegregation or in the vengeful behavior of a lynch mob, is motivated more by the fear of racial equality and economic threat that any other single factor. It is interesting to note that when economic conditions worsen, the incidence of lynching increases noticeably.

But that is not the whole story, because the element of frustration and the influence of other motivations are also discernible. The Nazis not only hated the Jews, but they hated and feared the "supremacy" of the Jewish people, just as the Japanese hated and feared the supremacy of the American people. In like manner, the Southerner in the United States is motivated by a passionate need to maintain white supremacy; when this need is frustrated by Supreme Court decisions, or the continuing emancipation of the Negro, his rage and hatred quickly spill over into acts of frightened violence. It is this need of different groups to maintain supremacy which gives the whole thing away. The passionate need to be superior exists only in those persons who feel insecure, inadequate, or inferior. If the Southern White felt secure within himself, if he really believed in his own superiority or supremacy, he would not be so easily frightened by the enhancement of the Negro's position. In these instances, then, it is the combined action of fear, inferiority, and frustration that leads to the outbreak of hostility and hatred.

There are several important characteristics of hostility that we should consider. The first of these is the tendency to generalize the attitude of hostility, and the second is the use of hostility for defensive purposes. The first characteristic is what makes hostility so dangerous in some instances and always damaging to interpersonal relationships. Let us remember, in trying to understand this generalization of hostility, that there is only a short distance between hating one's parents and despising mankind. We saw this fact sharply illustrated in the case of Bill, who felt that the whole human race "was no damned good." We see the same kind of generalization in racial prejudice, when from a single, unhappy experience with a Negro or a Jew or a Catholic, a person generalizes to the conclusion that all Negroes, Jews, and Catholics "are no damned good."

This is a common logical fallacy, and will be found in many different human relationships. In the case of a child generalizing from his attitude toward the parents, the generalization stems from the fact that for the child the parents are the most obvious prototypes of the human race. The child argues very simply that if you can't even trust your parents, then nobody can be trusted. If your parents can't love you, then how is it possible that your friends or neighbors should? In other instances, such as racial and religious hatred, the generalization is pegged to the fear that the hated group arouses in the person, and to the fact that it is safer and more convenient to project hostility to the entire group than it is to be selective and discriminating in one's judgments. Not to hate or mistrust the entire group would require individual evaluations and thus considerable mental effort. Besides, there is always the danger that one's evaluations could betray him and thus expose him to all of the hateful qualities which the enemy is known to possess. It is quite possible, so reasons the racial bigot, that an individual Jew might be a nice, reliable person; but it is much safer and more convenient to assume that this person, like the rest of the group, possesses the baleful or dangerous qualities that the group as a whole supposedly possesses.

This generalization of hostility and hatred, like the attitude itself, has obvious defensive advantages. Hostility can be and is used quite consistently to create and to maintain social distance between the hostile person and the people around him. Hostility keeps him from becoming involved in human relationships which he feels will always work (at least eventually) toward his detriment. It is better not to love (parents, friends, etc.) than to run the risk of getting hurt. In this way hostility becomes a person's Maginot Line, which permits

no penetration by other individuals. (See illustration.) Here,
again, we see how the anarchy of feeling dominates the
person's life and relationships, and effectively isolates him
from the world of people whom he wants so much to love.

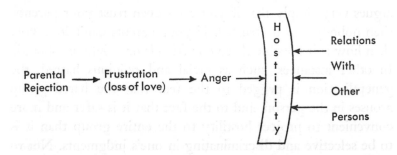

What are we to say about this dread aspect of the anarchy
of feeling, this mask of hatred that distorts the lives of so many
people? Must the unfortunate victim of hostility learn to
live with it? Is he doomed to a life of social isolation, a psychological leper living in the loneliness created by his hostility?
Or is it possible that the newly developed arts of counseling
and psychotherapy, skillfully wielded by an understanding
and accepting person, might break through the barrier and
reach the tormented soul of the victim?

Let us turn briefly to our friend Bill whom we introduced
at the start of this analysis. After many months of "working
through" his hatred of his parents, his hostility toward people
in general and his psychotherapist in particular, and continuously "ventilating" his feelings and experiences, Bill finally
reached the point where his hostility began to break down,
and he was able to see his parents in a much clearer light. Let
him tell you about it himself.

"I'm beginning to see that my hatred of my parents is an

ugly thing, and I no longer want any part of it. These feelings are beginning to disgust me. It scares the hell out of me to let go of them because they are the only safeguard I have had against being hurt by other people. But now I feel that I want to really love someone, particularly that girl I told you about. And I find that it is easier to talk to my parents. I feel more like doing something for them now instead of against them. The other night I surprised myself by doing the dishes for my mother so that she could go in and relax after dinner. What's more, I really wanted to, and I felt real good about it. There's a lot of the old feeling left, but I've learned that such feelings are very damaging, and that they have kept me from becoming the kind of person I should become. I think now that I can transcend these negative feelings and develop more positive ones toward other people."

In these few words we witness the breakdown of the anarchy of feeling, and the enthronement of the young man's higher powers of control. This is what he meant when he said that he could transcend these feelings and move in a more positive direction. This saga of a young man's commitment to hatred, and its eventual dissipation through psychotherapy, should teach us once and for all that the anarchy of feeling is a form of government that we should never accept. We should constantly rebel against this anarchy with whatever means and forces we can marshal in support of our efforts at self-government.

6 THE FRIGHTENED ONES

Fear is implanted in us as a preservative from evil;
but its duty, like that of other passions, is not to
overbear reason, but to assist it.

—JOHNSON.

IF ONE WERE to eavesdrop on the counseling sessions of a clinical psychologist or the therapeutic interviews of a psychiatrist, he would soon discover that the majority of the clients involved have one characteristic in common—they are anxious. Anxiety can be seen in their tense posture, in the perspiration that seeps out on their foreheads, in the constant shuffling of their legs, and in the ceaseless movement of their nervous fingers. It can be seen in the tone of their voice, their unaccountable fears, their attitudes toward life and reality, and in the many references to the threats and dangers of their daily existence.

"Doctor, I don't know what's wrong with me lately. I don't sleep well any more. I wake up in the middle of the night terribly frightened, as though some horrible nightmare had just occurred. My hands perspire continuously, I have a feeling of dread that something terrible is going to happen, I shudder with fear when I read stories about the hydrogen bomb, and all of the time there is this gnawing feeling of anxiety. I used to be so happy and carefree, and now my whole life seems poisoned with this awful fear."

These are the frightened ones, the countless thousands of

persons who live each day in a quagmire of uncertainty, insecurity, feelings of impending doom, and pervasive anxiety. Here, in sharp focus, we see the anarchy of feeling in one of its most destructive forms. It is not easy to live with constant fear as a companion. Fear, as we shall see, has its place in the scheme of things; but it is not meant to be chronic, anymore than a headache or a stomach pain (both of which are also danger signals) are supposed to be chronic. Constant, unremitting fear or anxiety is like intractable pain. It is intolerable, and always threatens to drive the unhappy victim to the edge of neurotic disintegration. Sometimes it pushes him over into the abyss of neurotic despair. This is what the textbooks refer to as an "anxiety neurosis," and what the man in the street quite often encounters as a "nervous breakdown." Chronic anxiety sits astride its hapless victim, and keeps prodding him until he collapses from sheer exhaustion.

What is this fear that is more than the fear of everyday experience? Why is it that some people can go through life relatively free of anxiety, while their fellow workers, or their wives or husbands, seem constantly beset with worry, uncertainty, and the feeling of insecurity? What is this chronic anxiety like as seen in the consulting room of the counselor or the psychotherapist?

Let us turn for a moment to the story of Jim. At the time he came for help, Jim was a young man just thirty years of age, planning to get married within six months to a woman six years his junior. Jim had been very successful in his work, was financially quite able to support a wife and family, and was very anxious to get married and have a family of his own. For years he had been burdened with the responsibility of his own immediate family, because his father was an alcoholic who failed to provide adequately for the family. Now, for the first time, Jim was able to consider the possibility of marriage seriously, and he was understandably anxious to make his dream come true.

But here the story changes hue. After becoming engaged, Jim became increasingly nervous and upset, complained of distress feelings in the stomach, and some rather frightening sensations in the chest cavity which convinced him that he was on the verge of a heart attack. These feelings of cardiac failure were intensified by the fact that several persons with whom he was closely associated succumbed to heart attacks at relatively early ages during the period that Jim was engaged. Jim was sure that he was going to die prior to his marriage, or that he would die shortly thereafter, leaving a widow and possibly even a child to survive the tragedy as best they could. This possibility increased his anxiety to the point where he was on the verge of panic.

"I can't figure out what it is, Doctor. I was always a healthy person, slept like a baby, ate like a horse, and haven't had a sick day in as long as I can remember. And now, after all of these years of hoping to get married some day, this has to come up. I don't know whether I should get married or not. I don't think it would be fair to my wife to get married and then drop dead. She's such a wonderful girl, and I wouldn't want to make a widow out of her, and possibly leave her with a child to support, within the first year or two after we got married. I just don't know what to do. I get these strong feelings of anxiety as though something terrible is going to happen, and then these pains in my chest start acting up. I'm sure that I am going to die. My stomach keeps acting up, too. I get these gas pains, and then I have to belch a lot, and sometimes I just don't eat for fear of my stomach acting up. Ann— that's my fiancée—is very patient and understanding with me, but I wouldn't blame her if she called the whole thing off. It must be sickening to hear a grown man like me complaining about his various pains, and acting like a frightened school boy.

"I just can't understand it. I have never been afraid of anything in my life. I started to work before I finished high school, and I have been on my own ever since. What's more, I've supported my mother for the past fourteen years, because my father is an alcoholic bum and can't keep a job. I've had to fight every inch of the way, and despite the fact that I never graduated from high school, I have a better income than most college graduates. In my work there is no place for pansies; you've got to be tough, and hard, and able to take it on the chin whenever things run against you. That's what's so puzzling about my condition. After all these years of taking care of myself in a tough, competitive world, and also taking care of my mother, I am acting like a teenager on his first date with not enough money to pay the check for dinner, or to get my girl home after a movie. I'm scared, and I don't know what I'm scared about. But I do know that if I don't get rid of this fear, I'll have to call the whole thing off, and Ann will be well rid of me."

Here we have a typical and a striking example of "the frightened ones." A grown man, toughened by the demands of growing up and caring for himself and his mother, and steeled by the daily effort to achieve success, Jim is nevertheless an anxious, frightened person in whom the prospect of getting married has aroused strong feelings of anxiety, which have in turn created deep uncertainties about himself, and have found an outlet in palpitations of the heart, chest pains, and stomach upset. Could it be that Jim was really afraid of getting married? Is it possible that he was backing away from the responsibilities of a wife and family, in view of the fact that he had clearly demonstrated for almost fifteen years that he was quite capable of assuming responsibility?

On the face of it this doesn't make sense. At the time that he was in counseling, Jim's salary was in the neighborhood of $20,000 a year, and showed promise of a steady increase. There was no question whatever that he was able to support a family. Moreover, he loved children, wanted a family of his own, and was extremely generous with his friends and loved ones. Jim was certainly not afraid of the responsibilities of marriage, nor was he tied to his mother's apron strings in such a way as to interfere with adequate marital relationships. Jim was quite willing to substitute Ann for his mother, even though in his generosity he had determined that his mother would also be cared for.

There is always the possibility in cases of this kind that the anxiety generated in connection with an impending marriage may reflect deep-seated sexual attitudes and relationships. No doubt, the Freudian would be quick to suggest that Jim's anxiety is obviously an expression of an unresolved Oedipal relationship, with its overtones of incest that certainly can cause a great deal of fear. This possibility must always be considered as a probable hypothesis in situations of this kind, and there was some evidence that Jim's relationship with his mother had some minor Oedipal overtones. And yet the evidence gathered from interview analysis, from free association, and from dream material was not enough to support this hypothesis. During the course of the counseling, Jim's relationship with his mother was worked through very thoroughly, leaving the conviction that this facet of his background played only a small part in determining his anxiety.

We shall have occasion a little later on to explore Jim's

background and experiences in order to find out where his anxiety came from, especially as it related to his impending marriage. But for the moment let us turn our attention to the nature and characteristics of anxiety, in order to avoid any possible misconceptions about the role of anxiety in a person's life. You are aware, of course, from your own experiences that anxiety in one form or another is a very common phenomenon, which appears periodically without regard for the personality, the emotional stability, or the health of the individual. You yourself have experienced anxiety many times, and until this moment may have given little thought to it, since it did not materially affect or alter the course of your life.

Characteristically, it appears in different guises, and it is not difficult to recognize the element of anxiety in such experiences as worry, apprehension, foreboding, and similar emotional states. All of these things are, at one time or another, a part of our lives, and if they are temporary and more or less superficial, we may pay them little heed. Yet we know from personal observation that the form of anxiety called worry can cause a great deal of trouble. The person who is worried about his health, his children's welfare, his job, his ability to support his family, pregnancy, or the successful completion of a college course, will sooner or later show the effects of worry. Such persons are tense, nervous, irritable, jumpy, and hard to get along with. They do not sleep too well, their digestion is impaired, they are often chronically constipated, find it hard to concentrate, and do not perform with the same efficiency that may have characterized their behavior prior to the onset of worry. The development of chronic worry is often the prelude to a full-blown anxiety neurosis, in which the individual is seriously incapacitated for coping with the demands of self or of reality, and for fulfilling the responsibilities of daily life.

And yet it would be a mistake to draw the inference from this that anxiety of itself is a detrimental or damaging emotion. It is quite natural and normal for a person to be anxious about an impending operation, a crucial examination, assuming new and more demanding responsibilities such as happen in marriage, the imminent birth of a child, or the changeover to a new and more complex job. It is theoretically possible for a person to possess so much security, self-confidence, and ego strength that nothing in his life phases him. He takes everything in stride without the least outward sign of anxiety or of worry. But if it happens at all, this is an extremely rare phenomenon, and certainly does not characterize the reactions of the great majority of people. As Henry Ward Beecher said, "God planted fear in the soul as truly as He planted hope and courage. It is a kind of bell or gong which rings the mind into quick life and avoidance on the approach of danger. It is the soul's signal for rallying."

One must understand that anxiety has its own teleology, that is, it serves a definite purpose in preserving or promoting the physical or psychological welfare of the individual. It is anxiety that prompts a sick person to consult a physician; it is anxiety that helps a student to get down to the business of studying; it is anxiety that prompts an employee to be on time for work and to do a good job; and it is anxiety that initiates the process of counseling. It is a basic axiom of both counseling and psychotherapy that a certain amount of anxiety is necessary in order to get counseling started and to keep it going; for without this anxiety the client is likely to discontinue the treatment and fall back on his own neurotic defenses and mechanisms in an effort to cope with reality.

Anxiety is essentially a form of fear, and fear is nature's danger signal by which the individual person is alerted to the fact that something is wrong and should be attended to, or that some danger is imminent and steps should be taken to cope with the threatening situation. Anxiety, therefore, is nature's safeguard against damage or destruction, and should be exploited for the good of the person by the practical application of safeguards or remedies. This is essentially the basic psychology of fear; and fear, like other natural emotions including love and anger, should be regarded as an asset of nature rather than as a liability.

It is not fear itself, but the fear that turns into excessive anxiety, worry, terror, or panic which is detrimental to good adjustment or mental health. Fear that has developed beyond control, as we see in the phobias, and fear that upsets the delicate balance of the human mind so that the person can no longer think clearly, or act prudently—such fear is detrimental to the welfare of the individual. This is what happens too often in the lives of people; but this does not mean that fear of itself is unhuman or irrational. One must always keep in mind that courage, one of the greatest of human virtues, is not the absence of fear; rather, it is the capacity to bring fear under integrative control. The courageous man knows the meaning of fear, but has developed the power to control it; the coward also knows the meaning of fear, but it controls him.

The existence of fear or anxiety, then, is not in itself a problem. But when it becomes chronic and pervasive, and when there seems to be little or no proportion between the feeling of anxiety and external events, the situation may quickly develop into a problem of sizable proportions. For example, a client once told me that he was quite worried about his sons' college education. I asked him how old the boys were, and he said two and four. In this little anecdote we see the rather startling disproportion between an external event and a person's anxiety. Admittedly, the cost of a college education today can arouse considerable anxiety when personal resources are limited; but not when the demand is only a part of the distant future.

Examples such as these, and there are countless others, indicate that the source of disturbing or disabling anxiety can be stimulated by external events or circumstances, just as in the case of normal anxieties. But they also suggest that the kind of anxiety developed will be determined less by the event itself than by the personality in which the anxiety develops. There is a great deal of difference between the person who worries about a college education for his children in the distant future and one who very thoughtfully sets up a savings or an endowment program which will provide resources for a college education later on. In the one case there is a morbid, unrealistic fear about the future, and in the other intelligent planning for the future. The psychology of fear, therefore, and the development of anxiety are directly related to individual personal characteristics. Whether the anxiety comes from without or from within one's self, its growth and its influence reflect the kind of personality one has developed throughout the years of childhood and adolescence.

The kind of anxiety we have been describing is related to normal anxiety insofar as it results from real-life situations. In these instances the anxiety is understandable, but it is out of all proportion to the character of the event that arouses it. The person is much more anxious than he should be at the time, which suggests of course that there are elements in his personality that act as stimulants to anxiety. In other instances, there is still another form of anxiety, which the textbooks describe as "free-floating." This is a good term for it because this kind of anxiety seems to have no anchor at all. There is nothing to which the anxiety can be specifically related—no impending event, no threatening situation, or no recent catastrophe. The person experiences a vague uneasiness, or a wave of anxiety, without knowing what he is anxious about. In such instances the subjective quality of the anxiety is quite apparent, and this gives us a clue to the origins of abnormal anxiety.

The victim of free-floating anxiety typically complains of various psychosomatic ailments. He does not sleep well; there is almost constant tension and fatigue; he may experience spells of dizziness, of cardiac palpitations, and of various other physical symptoms. Here again we see the anarchy of feeling at work within the personality. No amount of self-analysis, of insight, or of reasoning with one's self seems able to dispel this persistent, crippling feeling. This is the kind of anxiety our friend Jim experienced. It is true that he was on the verge of an important change in his life, involving the responsibilities of marriage and a family; and it is not at all uncommon for persons to experience some anxiety in connection with this impending responsibility. But Jim insisted repeatedly that the anxiety which he felt, and the symptoms connected with it, had very little to do with his impending marriage. He loved his fiancée deeply, he was accustomed to a great deal of responsibility and had been for a period of years, and he was financially solvent.

There is always, of course, the possibility that the anxiety in such cases would grow out of the sexual aspects of the relationship. I have seen many instances of this in my counseling experience as I am sure every other counselor or psychotherapist has. Women especially will react with anxiety as the hour of first sexual contact draws near. This anxiety may reflect a strong Jansenistic background in which sex was regarded as degrading, ugly, or evil; it may stem from a natural fear of the sex drive with its possibilites for disorganizing the personality; or it may result from uneasy misgivings regarding one's sexual status and identity. Very often the bride-to-be wonders if she is capable of sexual gratification and full orgastic response, whether her gifts of body will please her husband, or whether she can play the role of sex partner effectively. All of these misgivings about one's sexual potentialities can cause considerable anxiety.

But this anxiety is not limited to prospective wives. Men aspiring to be husbands are often plagued with deep feelings of uncertainty regarding their role as sexual partners. In my experience I have seen many instances of fears of sexual inadequacy, of possible impotence, and of organ deficiency. Many men have deep feelings of anxiety about their sexual potency and identity, and thus may experience typical anxiety symptoms as the wedding day approaches.

But this hypothesis was ruled out in the case of Jim. The most careful analysis failed to uncover any deep sexual anxieties. His image of himself, his clearly defined self-identity, and his experiences indicated conclusively that the anxiety which he felt did not originate in uncertainties regarding his sex role. Several interviews with his fiancée tended to confirm these impressions.

What, then, underlies this form of anxiety which seems to have no cause? Why does the unfortunate victim experience waves of anxiety when there is nothing to be anxious about? We know already that in these instances the anxiety comes from within the person himself, and thus we must look for the answer within the deeper recesses of the personality.

Inevitably we will find a deep, pervasive, *personal insecurity* which is woven into the basic makeup of the personality so that it becomes an integral part of the psychic structure and has much to do with determining the life-style of the person. In everything that he undertakes, in his interpersonal relationships, in his approach to responsibilities, in his attitude toward himself—the specter of insecurity can be seen in the background. It distorts his thoughts about himself, his strivings for realizable goals, and his attitudes toward the future. Because he feels deeply insecure *within himself*, the unhappy victim of this particular anarchy readily develops anxiety without external cause. He needs no threatening experiences or situations to touch off anxiety. Just to exist is threatening, because deep within himself is the conviction that he does not possess the resources necessary to cope with life and reality. It is like a man on the brink of a cliff with nothing to hold on to while a strong wind nudges him to the certain disaster that lies below. If only he could grab hold of something, and if only the wind would cease its inexorable push, he would be safe. But there is nothing, no secure foothold, no hand grip which he can use to stave off the impending disaster, and thus he experiences wave upon wave of crippling anxiety.

Let us return to the story of Jim in order to illustrate this type of psychic makeup. You will recall our mentioning earlier that Jim's father was a habitual drinker, who lost job after job, and failed miserably to provide for his family. This type of situation is likely to breed deep feelings of insecurity, not only because it blocks the essential needs for physical welfare and safety, but also because it involves a great deal of internal family conflict and dissension that threatens the stability and the integrity of the home. This sort of situation always spells danger to a young child, and he begins to see the world as a place of constant danger and threat. He begins to feel insecure; and because he is young and does not yet possess the resources necessary to cope adequately with the demands and threats of reality, the insecurity of the situation becomes internalized as a feeling of insecurity within himself. This is exactly what happened to Jim.

In addition, there was the fact that Jim had to assume adult responsibilities when still quite young. Because the father failed to provide adequately, Jim had to take over the financial responsibility for the home. This early assumption of adult responsibilities by a child often has detrimental effects on ego-formation, for the simple reason that the load is too heavy. The youngster cannot help wondering whether he will be able to carry this load. With a self still in the process of formation, he is not at all sure that he possesses the resources necessary to fulfill the responsibilities imposed on him, and thus the feeling of insecurity is reinforced by additional demands. In Jim's case, he actually fulfilled these demands quite creditably, but the price that he paid was too high. As he grew older, and developed more confidence in his ability to handle the demands of everyday life, he repressed these early feelings of insecurity, but they continued to ferment below the surface and finally erupted in a free-floating anxiety.

To complicate matters, Jim was drafted into the service, and despite the fact that he had not graduated from high school, he was quickly promoted from the ranks to a position of command. Again he was faced with overwhelming responsibility for which he did not feel personally equipped. Nevertheless, he played the role to perfection and gave every appearance of the self-assured, courageous, and competent officer. However, deep within himself he was frightened by the terrible responsibility for the lives of the men under his command, and he developed an almost uncontrollable fear of death. Along with this, he developed a deep sense of guilt whenever one of his men was killed, and he began to feel that his number would come up very soon. He argued to himself that it was only fair that he too should be killed since so many men for whom he was responsible had already died. He developed the obsession that he was living on borrowed time, and thus death was always nearby, ready to point its finger at him. It is for this reason that he reacted so disastrously to the death of people whom he knew. Their death was a reminder that his own was long overdue. The path of insecurity had come full circle, since death, which is the ultimate proof of insecurity, waited only for the right moment.

It was this intimate association with the concept and probability of death that led to Jim's attacks of anxiety. Possessed for many years by deep feelings of insecurity, and convinced that he was already living on borrowed time, he viewed marriage as a frightening possibility. He saw himself as collapsing just before the wedding ceremony was to take place. The idea that he would die soon after getting married, thus depriving his wife of the things she wanted so much, became a nightmare to him. Uncertainty piled on uncertainty, and indecision became a daily torture. Jim's early insecurity, nurtured by heavy responsibilities, and prodded by the awful probabilities of combat, had finally spawned a full-blown anxiety neurosis. Jim was not afraid of everyday responsibilities, or of the demands of marriage. He was literally afraid to live, and this is the ultimate outcome of the anarchy of feeling represented by insecurity.

This particular instance of the anarchy of feeling is not limited to the unfortunate and unhappy Jims of the world. It is a disease that has spread to many parts of the world and has infected millions of people. Nowhere, perhaps, is it more clearly evident than in America. Not too long ago, self-reliance was an outstanding characteristic of most Americans. They took care of themselves, their families, and their own futures. But now the emphasis seems to have swung to security in place of self-reliance. Applicants for jobs seem to be more interested in pension plans than in opportunities for personal growth or challenge. College seniors harass the placement office from the first day of their senior year in an ill-concealed anxiety about what is going to happen after graduation. Insurance companies report profits of astronomical proportions. Unemployment benefits are doled out to millions of workers out of jobs. Government subsidies aimed at guaranteeing the security of various groups run into the billions of dollars. Scholarships, assistantships, government loans, and grants of various kinds are made available to thousands of college and university students in a frantic effort to promote and even guarantee their academic security. In every direction, the signs are the same—security is the watch-word of existence, and the need for security outranks all others in dynamic impact.

These tell-tale signs of the feelings of insecurity (or, what is the same thing, an increased need for security) indicate with a brilliant clarity that a new dimension in personality dynamics has been taking shape. It is an interesting fact that, prior to World War I, psychological treatises had little to say about the need for security, although the concept was reflected in the instinct for self-preservation. Today, it is generally recognized among psychological and social theorists that the individual anxiety revealed on the analytic couch or in the counseling room has its counterpart in a generalized, almost universal anxiety among the masses of people who inhabit the earth. This psychological-social development has its roots in certain historical events which have tended to undermine personal self-reliance, the feeling of security, stable and permanent value systems, and the conviction of safety that characterized people of a generation or two ago. Thus the individual factors that breed the feeling of insecurity, as we saw in the case of Jim, are complemented by a host of social influences that have raised mass cowardice to a new high.

One need not look far into the recent past to find a number of events which have induced a generalized anxiety. Prominent among these events are the two World Wars with their threat of massive and widespread destruction, the great depression of the thirties, the displacement of large groups of people because of emigration, war, agrarian changes, and shifting economic demands and opportunities, the profound changes in the social-sex status of women, the disintegration of the family, and the disruption of basic value systems because of the inroads made by pragmatism, hedonistic thinking, psychoanalysis, and existential philosophy. These historical events have tended to undermine the feeling of security by posing a threat to individual existence and personal worth, thus giving rise to widespread anxiety. In this manner, threat, anxiety, and insecurity come together to produce the typical, familiar picture of the timid, frightened personality.

It is important for us to realize that when internal, personal security is threatened or disrupted by external forces like those already mentioned, several things are likely to happen and actually have happened in the past generation. First of all, under the impetus of the intense anxiety that results from loss of security, people turn to external sources for security rather than searching for and finding it within themselves.

Hence the popularity of "social security" programs, retirement benefits, mutual stock plans, outlandish insurance policies, and get-rich-quick schemes. Hence, too, the supine and somewhat amazing complacency regarding inflation, until we recall that inflation represents higher wages as well as higher prices. And higher wages, of course, are regarded as a boon to security.

This ceaseless search for security in programs and panaceas external to the self has an almost infantile quality. It reminds us of the infant's complete dependency on the mother for succor, safety, satisfaction, and security. Supposedly this symbiotic relationship between mother and infant lays the groundwork for ego-security in later life. Thus, under conditions of extreme threat and disorganization, society becomes the symbolic mother-figure at the breast of whom individual members continue to suckle for most of their lives, including the period of retirement.

This projection of the source of security into the social structure inevitably weakens individual security and dissipates the personal self in exactly the same manner that the personality fails to achieve wholeness and integration when the symbiotic relationship between mother and child is projected beyond infancy into adolescence and adulthood. While this relationship is required for the launching of individual security, future freedom from anxiety also requires emancipation from, and independence of, maternal control. People must discover that the only true security is the security that exists within themselves. It cannot be bought with higher wages or with insurance plans, nor can it be engrafted on the servile man by a paternalistic government. Until people become aware of this fundamental truth regarding human personality, the anarchy of insecurity and anxiety will continue to prevail.

We must understand that the feeling of insecurity stems from a number of sources, and not just from the threat to safety. This reminds us that its psychological opposite, security, assumes several different forms, the dynamic background of which may vary considerably from person to person. Thus security is related by different writers to the needs for status, safety, love, and survival; and, because of the obvious implications of these needs for emotional stability or health, it is most often referred to as "emotional security." From a psychological point of view, then, security is most often defined as a feeling-quality which promotes the conviction of safety, status, and personal worth, and insures the ability to cope successfully with life's demands, threats, conflicts, and frustrations. When, therefore, a child is unloved, rejected, or made to feel unwanted or hated, his feeling of self-esteem and personal worth is shattered and he begins to feel deeply insecure. To be loved, and able to accept and give love, are necessary ingredients for the growth of the sense of security; without them adequate adjustment and mental health are not likely to develop.

Of the various personal qualities to which the feeling of security is related, one of the most basic is the feeling of safety. The feeling of safety is more directly related to the physical welfare and integrity of the person, and is most clearly expressed as freedom from threat or danger; on the other hand, psychological or emotional security develops more directly from acceptance, approval, love, and belonging.

Nevertheless, the intimate relationship between physical safety and security is exemplified clearly in cases of traumatic neuroses. In these cases, which strongly resemble the anxiety reactions of the insecure person, there is always a background of real injury, or the threat of injury and death. Typically, the symptoms develop after some incident that is interpreted by the person as a threat to his physical existence. In one such case observed by the writer, the client had been involved in a serious automobile accident, which might have caused his death, but from which he miraculously escaped without injury. Following this disturbing experience (psychic trauma), he developed the typical symptoms of excessive perspiration, unusual sensitivity, irritability, and dizziness. These symptoms were especially acute if he had to use an automobile for transportation. Perhaps the most characteristic symptom in such cases is the terrifying nightmare in which the patient relives again and again the traumatic experience that touched off the neurotic development.

The important lesson to learn from such cases is that the threat to physical safety and to life itself can produce effects essentially similar to the anxiety that stems from the feeling of insecurity. In fact, the traumatic event that touches off the reaction is interpreted by the person as a threat to personal security. Suddenly, the world is dangerous, threatening, full of impending death. The traumatic incident seems to force him to a realization that he is incapable of contending with the forces of life and death. His extreme reaction to a threatening situation shows that he not only has a deep need for physical safety, but that there is also a feeling of insecurity which existed even before the traumatic incident. Here, in a dramatic way, the common neurotic characteristic of helplessness is exemplified very clearly. Here, too, the anarchy of feeling appears in one of its most vivid forms.

This relationship between basic needs and dynamic feelings that often dominate a person's life is one that counseling and psychotherapy have taught us to expect. Whenever critical personality needs are not gratified, or are inadequately fulfilled, we can look for some disturbance in the person's emotional life. Security itself is a need, and the adequate fulfillment of this need will lead to the feeling of security. But this basic need is also interlocked with other personality requirements, particularly love and affection, belonging, status, and safety. Therefore, the feeling of security, or of insecurity will be deeply affected by whatever happens to all of these critical needs. This is exactly what happened in the case of Jim, whose general experience is repeated in countless other situations where the feeling of insecurity has gained a strangelhold on the personality, and anxiety has become a constant companion.

What is the probable outcome when the anarchy of feeling takes this particular form? Is there any possibility of reestablishing reason on its rightful throne? Is it possible through counseling or psychotherapy to dispel the crippling anxiety that is caused by insecurity? These are difficult questions to answer, and any answer would have to be qualified by reference to a number of conditions that would affect the process and the outcome of any treatment. Anyone risking an answer to these questions would want to know something about the organization of the client's personality, how long the anxiety had persisted, his attitude towards himself and reality, the quality of other need-gratifications, and so on.

The results of counseling are always determined by a great many factors, not the least of which is the personality and skill of the counselor. If we use the case of Jim as something of a yardstick, it is interesting to note that he overcame his anxiety to a point where he was able to go through with his wedding plans, has been successfully married for the last three years, and in a follow-up interview reported that the psychosomatic symptoms which had brought him to counseling occurred only infrequently and with far less intensity than before. There is still a great deal of insecurity in Jim's makeup, but in the course of counseling he developed a healthy insight into the background of his insecurity, and into the relationship between these feelings and the anxiety attacks. He has also accepted the fact that his "heart attacks" and other physical symptoms were psychosomatic and did not signify impending death. Undoubtedly, there are many similar cases in the files of counselors and psychotherapists in which there has been a partial or complete remission of disabling symptoms, and these cases certainly encourage us to believe that the anarchy of feeling which plagues the lives of frightened people can be dissipated by enlisting the support of reason. As Samuel Johnson remarked, "All fear is painful, and when it conduces not to safety, it is painful without use. Every consideration, therefore, by which groundless terrors may be removed adds something to human happiness."

7 THE FAULTY IMAGE

The most difficult thing in life is to know yourself.

—THALES.

WHEN DAVE first came to see me, he seemed like dozens of other normal, healthy college youngsters who have run into the age-old problem of deciding on a career. This is one of the most common problems that high school and college counselors encounter in their daily work, and would ordinarily evoke nothing more than a sincere professional interest in helping a young man formulate realizable goals toward which he could strive in an efficient and intelligent manner. But there was something about Dave's manner that suggested that his problem ran deeper than the ordinary vocational uncertainty. He was a good-looking, well-built young man who might well have come in looking for a story for the college paper. But there was an obvious undertone of tension manifested in the washboard wrinkles of his forehead, the too-erect position as he sat facing me, and the ceaseless winding and unwinding of his fingers. I waited for him to start talking.

In an obvious effort to control his feelings and to organize his thoughts, Dave began to tell me why he had sought the help of a counselor. Smiling somewhat nervously, he said, "I almost didn't keep my appointment today, then I thought I had better get it over with. I suppose you will think I am a bit foolish coming to you with such a problem when there are so many others with more serious difficulties, but this thing is beginning to get me down and I need some help. I can't seem to lick it by myself. I have talked to my parents, my friends, and to just about anybody who will listen, but I haven't gotten anywhere. Do you think you can help me?" I waited for a moment before answering, and then suggested that if he would tell me what the problem was I would be glad to do what I could. At that Dave broke into a rather sheepish grin, realizing that he had talked about the problem but had forgotten to mention what it was.

"I guess I'm so nervous coming to see a psychologist that I can't think straight. Anyway, while I am not at all sure that it is a serious problem, I'm pretty worried about my future. Here I am a senior in college, with a major in economics, and I haven't the faintest idea what I am going to do when I graduate, or what I should do. I realize that there are a lot of guys in the same boat, but that doesn't help me any. What's worse, a lot of the fellows I know have decided on their careers, and some of them made up their minds when they were in freshman or sophomore year. But somehow I have never been able to figure out what I should do. I majored in economics because a business career seemed the most likely possibility, but I might as well have majored in English or in Sanskrit for what good it has done me. I have no more interest in becoming a business man than in being a teacher, or a writer, or something else."

With the floodgates down, Dave went on with his story in a torrent of words which reflected the tension and anxiety that had finally brought him to the counseling center. "I haven't really the faintest idea why I majored in economics. At one time I thought it would be English, then I got interested for a while in sociology, and finally elected economics mainly because some friends of mine suggested that it would be a good background for a business career. Besides, my father is a Wall Street broker and I know that he would like me to get interested in some phase of business.

"But I can't see myself in the business world. In fact, I can't see myself in any kind of a vocational role. Whenever I try to think of doing something like banking, selling insurance, working in a brokerage office, or getting up reports for some business firm, my mind seems to go blank. I just can't seem to see myself in those roles. As a matter of fact, I can't seem to see myself in any of the roles that older people play, especially after they get out of college. I went steady with a girl once, but I quit when she got serious, because I couldn't see myself being married to anyone. I wouldn't know how to act like a husband, and Lord knows I certainly wouldn't know how to act like a father. I guess I'm just destined to be a nonentity, because that certainly is the way I feel inside. There doesn't seem to be any real me. When I try to think of who I am, or what I'm supposed to be, or what I'm supposed to do in this life, I draw a complete blank. It's got me real worried. I'll be graduating in a few months, and for the life of me I don't know what I am going to do. Can you help me? Are there any tests or something that you could give me to help me find out what my real vocation is? I sure hope you can help me."

In these poignant, almost tragic questions of a young man searching desperately for self, we see the anarchy of feeling working in still another dimension of the human mind, that is, the dimension of self-identity. Unfortunately, as with other instances that we have studied, there are thousands upon thousands of people involved in this endless search for a self that seems somehow constantly to elude their grasp. Time after time the psychological counselor hears the same refrain, even though it is expressed in different words: "I've always felt that I was in the wrong vocation; I should have been a lawyer." "Even though I am forty years old, I've never really found myself." "I've never been able to stick at anything for any period of time. After a while, I get bored by my job and look for something else." "I think I'll go to California. Maybe there I will find what I am looking for." "I've never gotten married because I was never sure that I would be a good wife or mother." "I've never really found myself in all these years, but I think this new job will do it." And so goes the refrain of uncertainty, confusion, indecisiveness, lack of direction, and anxiety—a refrain that always ends on one note— a deep, pervasive feeling of non-identity.

The unhappy victims of the failure to achieve self-identity are found in all walks of life. There is, for example, the unhappy and miserable wife who has never defined for herself what her role should be. Whether in the marriage bed, in the kitchen, or entertaining her husband's friends, she is always uncertain and anxious about enacting her role. In the embrace of her ardent husband, she feels strange and alienated, feeling that this should not be happening to her, or perhaps that it is happening to someone else. In her attempts to mother her children and to care for their deepest needs, she feels clumsy and inept, and she begins to long for the freedom that was hers in bygone days when she was not required to enact such precise roles. In everything she does, there is a feeling of emptiness and self-alienation, because she finds it impossible to project her unknown self into the roles she is expected to play.

There is also the hapless and confused husband who is strangely embarrassed by his wife's nudity, or by the demands of his children that he should act like a father. For reasons unknown to himself, he turns away while his wife disrobes, and he feels a strange uneasiness when her warmth and passion reach out to him with the intimate language of sexual love. He strives hard to enact the role of father, but he soon finds the attentions and demands of the children irritating and confusing. He wants to relate to them but there is a mysterious barrier that stops him from playing the role effectively. He probably experiences vague and uneasy feelings of unmanliness, of lacking the virile masculinity that would enable him to reach out toward and embrace his wife and children, and to assume the responsibilities and the leadership that family living requires.

Like the wife who lacks self-identity, he finds it difficult to project himself into roles that society expects him to assume; and he longs for the bygone freedom in which such demands did not exist. The ultimate tragedy that stems from this anarchy of feeling takes shape when he finds that, after six or eight or ten years of marriage, he is suddenly and strangely impotent, no longer able to maintain the fiction that he had zealously guarded for so many years. Now he stands exposed to both himself and his wife—an empty shell of a person in whom the qualities of masculinity and self-identity have dissipated in the strenuous effort to maintain a fictional role that had little substance from the very start.

A typical instance of this failure to maintain the fiction of masculinity because of non-identity is the case of a man we will call Jerry. When Jerry first came to counseling some years ago, he was a tall, rangy young man who clearly reflected the Southwest from which he came. He and his wife had just celebrated their sixth wedding anniversary, which happened to coincide with the birth of their second child. Jerry told his tale of woe in a very few minutes. He and his wife, a strikingly attractive brunette, had been happily married until his loss of interest in her as a sexual partner initiated the estrangement. There was not only loss of interest but a continually developing impotence which had reached the point where sexual relationships had disappeared completely. On her part, the wife turned from her husband in disappointment and disgust, at which point the estrangement became complete, and their obvious conflict began to affect the behavior of the children.

What Jerry first noticed was a dying out of the flame that had drawn him to his wife physically—a flame, however, that had never flickered too strongly. Characteristically, Jerry stated that he had never been comfortable in his role of husband and father, even though he loved both his wife and his children. "I just don't know how to act in these situations. I know that my wife expects me to be an ardent lover, but actually this physical intimacy embarrasses me. I guess that's one of the reasons why I became impotent. Perhaps I figured subconsciously that if I became impotent I wouldn't have to go through the farce of sexual relationships any more. I realize that my wife is sexually attractive, and that she needs the physical expression of love very deeply, but I'm just not interested."

He hesitated for a while and then went on with his unhappy story. "I feel much the same way about the children. I love them in an objective sort of way, but I don't really feel like a father toward them. I don't know what a father is supposed to be like. They come to me with their problems and questions, or just to be loved, and I act like a stranger toward them. In fact, I sometimes feel like a stranger in my own home. I don't know how to do things around the house, I repeatedly forget to pay the bills, and I often think how wonderful it would be just to be by myself without the entangling relationships that marriage involves. I know that I am a horrible disappointment to my wife, but there isn't anything that I can do about it."

You can see how similar are the two cases we have described, despite the fact that on the surface they have very different characteristics. Dave is vocationally disoriented, and Jerry is a marital misfit. Yet, it is clear from an analysis of their feelings that both are wrestling with the same problem—the failure of self-identity. These two unhappy people are rather striking representatives of a large group of persons suffering in one degree or another from the same confusion and anxiety. In the religious life, for example, there are many men and women who have not been able to find themselves. In fact, one of the strongest motives for entering the service of God is the belief among many aspirants that here at last they will find what they are looking for. In the close union with God they are sure "to find themselves." However, the unusually high dropout rate among aspirants to the religious life indicates with striking clarity how ill-founded this belief often is. The number of broken lives, and the vast accumulation of discouragement and disillusionment resulting from this mistaken belief, are testimony to the fact that any vocation by itself, whether religious or lay, will not guarantee the discovery of self. Self-identity is a quality of the human person that should be acquired in the course of normal development by the time the adolescent reaches the vestibule of adulthood. As we shall see, it is forged in the crucible of experience and maturation, and nurtured by interpersonal relationships; and this process should be nearly completed by the time that a person is ready to formulate life goals.

The anarchy of feeling which reflects the failure to achieve self-identity reaches into other phases of adult life besides the marital and religious. There are countless persons in the business and professional worlds, as well as in the sphere of arts and letters, who find it difficult or impossible to enact their roles with any degree of efficiency or satisfaction. This is one of the reasons why job frustration is so widespread, and it also explains the almost frantic effort of people in all walks of life to escape into the oblivion of alcoholic stupor, incessant social activities, or a stupefying hobby that transports them to a world of dreams and fantasies.

There is little doubt that many actors and actresses are lured into the dramatic field by the promise of finding themselves in one or another of the roles they portray on the stage, only to end up in a state of complete confusion. The fact that many of them have failed to achieve self-identity is luridly illustrated in the sordid record of separations, divorces, endless quarreling, and multiple marriages. The kings and queens of that never-never land called Hollywood have written a vivid history of the anarchy of feeling that is associated with non-identity. The unremitting search for the "right" mate, the endless, stupefying pleasure-seeking, the migration to other parts of the world, and similar behavior dramatize the failures of these wretched souls to find the core of their own being.

A similar picture could be drawn for business and professional people, but both clinical experience and casual observation suggest that professional persons—doctors, lawyers, engineers, and clergymen—have less difficulty in this regard because of the focalizing effect of their professions. College educators will attest to the fact that youngsters who are strongly oriented toward a particular profession in the early years of their college life seem to be much surer of their direction, less confused, and more strongly self-identified than those who have no vocational aspirations, or who aspire to non-professional fields. It is quite probable that the early achievement of self-identity has a strong influence on the kind of vocation that is chosen.

The failure to achieve self-identity is perhaps most clearly exemplified in the more extreme forms of sexual confusion, particularly homosexuality. It is important for us to recognize that sexual confusion can range all the way from the uncertainty about sexual status experienced by the young adolescent through varying degress of inadequate masculinity and effeminacy up to the threshold of latent and overt homosexuality. In all such instances the effort to achieve self-identity will be impeded to some extent; but it is obvious that actual homosexuality not only impedes self-identity but tends to exclude it altogether.

The relation between sexual confusion and the failure of self-identity is so obvious as to require little comment or explanation. If a person is so confused that he cannot identify with the basic role involved in masculinity or femininity, then, certainly, to be sure of what he is or what he is supposed to become will be a formidable task. Whenever a person has serious doubts about his sex status, and begins to wonder whether he possesses qualities of or belongs to, the opposite sex, it becomes impossible for him to project himself (or herself) into roles in which masculinity or femininity play an essential part. Quite typically, homosexuals find it impossible to project themselves into the role of a sexual partner where the opposite sex is concerned. They find it difficult or extremely distasteful to initiate the process of dating or of going steady. They eschew all heterosexual exploration. And they find it impossible to think of themselves in the role of a husband or father. This is sexual confusion at its worst, and it is another striking example of how the anarchy of feeling can serve to disrupt and to distort the lives of its hapless victims.

We must not let the important fact slip away from us at this point that the lesser degrees of sexual confusion are probably much more common than overt homosexuality, and that often these confused feelings lie at the basis of the inexplicable behavior and attitudes of people that so often puzzle us. The sudden destruction of the "perfect" marriage, the unbelievable change of jobs, the irritating uncertainty and indecision that some people manifest in numerous situations, the breaking off of a long engagement, or the continuous shifting from one job to another, are in many instances the result of inadequate self-identity. This fact is clearly illustrated in the case of the young woman who broke off three different engagements and has never married to this day. Although very attractive, well-dressed, and of unusually good breeding, her lack of self-identity made it impossible for her to accept the relationship of marriage, and to project herself into the roles that she would be expected to play as a married woman. She could not accept the implications that being a wife involved, nor could she tolerate the thought of motherhood. And thus was she doomed to wander aimlessly through life looking for that most elusive of commodities—the self.

In all of these examples of non-identity and the search for self, whether in mild form or extreme, the signs are very similar. There is always the uncertainty, the role confusion, poorly defined or non-existent goals, sexual confusion, indecision, and of course a certain amount of unhappiness, discontent, and anxiety. There is also the restless search for a focal point that would give some direction to personal strivings and some more precise meaning to life itself. And there is something of a feeling of being isolated, apart from the group, and different from one's fellow human beings. These secondary feelings fit into the total anarchy of feeling and thus contribute their own dynamic quality to the disruption of the unfortunate victim's peace of mind and contentment. We see this clearly illustrated in the case of Dave whose confusion, disorientation, and lack of goals had brought him to the edge of emotional disequilibrium.

What is this feeling of self-identity that seems to be so basic to achieving the good things in life? Where does it come from, and why do some people fail to achieve it? The feeling or conviction of self-identity can be described very simply as knowing *who* we are, *what* we are, and *where* we are going. It is the firm conviction that at the center of my being there is an I or ego or self that is clearly defined in my own mind, that possesses sharp boundaries which distinguish it from other selves, and that has a way of projecting itself into the center of things that directly concern me.

Possessing self-identity, I am keenly aware that self is the center of my personal existence, and that all things concerning my life are centered on this self. Moreover, they are integrated into it in such a way as to form a unified whole rather than a disunified conglomerate of feelings, experiences, attitudes, and aspirations. It is this integrated unity of self that lies at the basis of self-identity and selfhood, and this unity precludes or dissipates the confusion, the uncertainty, and the indecision that occur when the self is a loosely organized mosaic. This is what we mean by the flat affirmation: "I know who I am, and I know what I am."

Selfhood has its beginnings very early in life, is sharply delineated through the tribulations and other experiences of adolescence, and usually assumes its more or less final form in early adulthood. This, at least, is as it should be, but there are many factors that thwart such normal development. In infancy and early childhood, if all goes well, the ego or I gradually becomes differentiated from the rest of the world, and the young child, pulsating with the energy of life and eagerly absorbing each new experience, finally comes to know himself as distinct from other persons. He becomes *self*-conscious rather than world-conscious, at which time he typically abandons the third person reference, which is so characteristic of young children, in favor of the "I" reference. There has gradually emerged within the core of experience a focal point to which distinctively personal things are henceforth referred as belonging to himself. He has become a self-conscious being with a distinctively personal existence.

This period of ego development is of profound significance for the future well-being of the child, because if the ego fails to develop or to become sharply differentiated from outer reality, the unfortunate victim is deprived of effective means of coping with reality. Such persons are passive, confused, and dependent individuals who never achieve self-identity in the full sense of the term, and who find it impossible to take their rightful place in the sun. You can well understand that without an ego or self there can be no self-identity: and it is often in the early stages of development that the failure to achieve self-identity takes root.

Instances of this type of development failure are encountered regularly in counseling and psychotherapy. Let us look in for a moment on the life of Rita, a small, dark girl of Polish descent. At the time that she came into counseling, she was twenty-one years of age and had recently begun graduate studies in English. She complained of being unable to concentrate, to keep up with class assignments, and to achieve a passing grade. These complaints were particularly significant in view of the fact that she had a high I.Q. and had graduated *cum laude* from a prominent university.

We are not interested here in the probable diagnosis of schizophrenia, but rather in Rita's very inadequate ego development. You had to be with her only a short time to sense the weakness of her personal self and to become aware of the poorly defined boundaries of her inner personality. Like all people with a defective ego formation, she could not express her thoughts clearly, was uncertain of her feelings at any particular moment, and found it difficult to organize her psychic life around a definite aim or goal. Similarly, because of the diffusion of identity, she could not relate effectively to other people and found it extremely uncomfortable to carry on an ordinary conversation and to meet other social demands. It did not take long to find out that Rita's early development was marked by emotional starvation. Her immigrant parents had no idea of how to relate effectively to their love-hungry daughter, and thus Rita's ego could not take definite form. Hence, at twenty-one, Rita was still starved for affection; she could not relate effectively to people, and showed a noticeable lack of self-identity.

The developmental failure that plagued this unfortunate girl illustrates an important facet of the growth of self-identity. Just as the ego must take form and provide the groundwork for self-conscious existence during the first five or six years of the child's life, so for self-identity there must be some significant person or persons with whom the child can identify in an intimate, nourishing relationship that will give his ego an added thrust toward self-identity. It is these growing relationships that help the young child to define the boundaries of his own self. We need hardly add that if the relationship is pushed too far by an over-possessive parent, self-identity will again become diffused and the boundaries of self will become blurred and indistinct. Too much love, like too little, always interferes with adequate ego development.

Before pursuing this trend of thought further, we must bring in a basic element in the growth of self-identity—an element so basic, in fact, that without it self-identity is impossible. What we are referring to is *sex-identity*, which by its very nature constitutes the core of self-identity. You can easily understand from your own growth experiences that unless a person perceives himself clearly and unmistakably as male or as female, he is blocked from knowing what he is or what he is supposed to be. Moreover, this obscure sex-identity will invariably prevent him (or her) from projecting himself into future roles that are inseparably bound up with masculinity or femininity. If I do not see myself as a man, I certainly cannot see myself as a future husband, father, or lover. Similarly, if my perceptions of myself as a woman are obscure or confused, I will find it impossible to project myself into the roles of wife, mother, or sexual partner. The conviction of masculinity or of femininity is the prerogative of every man or woman. What is more, it is a psychological necessity if the person is to live a fully adequate adult life.

This clear perception and unshakable affirmation of masculinity or femininity constitute the essential core of self-identity around which other identifications become organized into the pattern of self-identity. It is for this reason that the formation of the body image plays such a prominent role in the growth of sex status and the achievement of self-identity.

That a poorly formed body image can undermine sex status and sex roles is manifested in numerous case studies. For example, one such client felt that her breast development was inadequate to establish the physical contours that she felt a woman must possess in order to be attractively feminine. This so affected her feeling about herself and her own femininity that her sex relationships with her husband were seriously undermined. The interesting fact in this case is that the young woman's physical contours were in good proportion so that her figure was quite attractive. In other words, the *image* that she formed of her psysical makeup was distorted and unrealistic, and it was this image rather than the reality which disturbed her feelings about herself as a woman.

The same sort of body image distortion is seen in many men who are convinced that their sexual apparatus is inadequate for the achievement of sexual gratification or for satisfying the needs of a sexual partner. This generally takes the form of imagining that the penis is much smaller than the average, and this conviction regarding the body leads directly to feelings of inadequacy about being completely masculine. In one such instance this feeling persisted despite the fact that the man and his wife had had satisfactory sex relationships for a period of six years and had four children. This type of persistent attitude, based on a failure to achieve complete self-identity, shows how the anarchy of feeling can dominate reason. No matter what the facts are, and regardless of the demands of logic, feelings often manage to dominate human reason.

The role of the body image in the gradual emergence of self-identity demonstrates how important it is to develop healthy attitudes toward our physical self, including the sexual apparatus. This is particularly true in adolescence, when the body image is often distorted by temporary physical imperfections due to deep-seated changes taking place within the physical structure, or because the adolescent has developed a distorted picture of what he is actually like. Especially serious is the failure of the adolescent to develop an adequate sex-identity, not only because of his feelings and images regarding his physical self, but even more importantly because of other developmental failures or mistakes that often occur during adolescence. Failing to see and to understand himself as a man, and lacking the deep conviction of masculinity, he enters into a period of confusion and disorientation which interferes seriously with vocational choices and future role identifications. We saw this clearly in the case of Dave, who could not decide on a vocational goal, and we saw it again in the case of Jerry, who found it impossible to continue enacting the role of husband and father. Let us say it again, because it bears repeating: Without the deep conviction of masculinity or femininity, a man or woman cannot function effectively as an adult, nor can he build a secure and healthy pattern of interpersonal relationships which adult roles always involve.

Granted that a secure body image and a healthy sex identity provide a tremendous thrust toward self-identity, what other elements in a person's life does the counselor or therapist find which would either favor or impede the emergence of self-identity? We have already referred to the importance of early interpersonal relationships in the process of ego formation during childhood. Let us now return to a study of these relationships and try to find out what additional implications they have for the growth of self-identity. Left to his own devices, the child might acquire a feeling of self-identity through his own natural endowments. After all, the boy has a natural push toward masculinity and sex status as a male, and the girl a similar push toward femininity. We have taken note of this fact in our reference to the body image.

However, this isn't the way things happen in actuality. The

child, in order to gain ego strength and security, tends naturally to identify with one or another parent in his immediate environment. Because they are deeply alike in certain respects, the boy then will tend to identify with the father (if one is available), and the girl with the mother. This sort of natural, positive identification provides an additional push toward the achievement of sex identity, since the object of identification possesses certain traits that the child can assimilate to himself. The more masculine the father, or the more feminine the mother, the more certainly will the youngster realize the fruits of self-identity. This type of identification often carries over into adulthood, as we see very clearly in boys who "follow in their father's footsteps," or in girls who strive to emulate their mothers.

But what happens when this positive identification does not take place, because of absence of the father, defection on the part of the mother, parental rejection of the child, favoritism, jealousy, or a host of other situations and relationships that serve to throttle any effort at identification? What if the boy identifies with the mother, or the girl with the father, causing what the textbooks call "cross-identification"? We can well imagine that something rather terrible is going to happen if the masculinity of the boy gets mixed up with the femininity of the mother, or the femininity of the daughter is suppressed by identification with the father. The outcome of this sort of relationship will of course depend upon the degree of identification, but we can be sure that in many instances there will be a great deal of sexual confusion, failure of sex-identity, and serious difficulties in fulfilling certain sex roles. The basis of confusion regarding one's self is the development of ambivalent feelings and attitudes regarding sex status. This ambivalence of feelings and attitudes is clearly exemplified in the latent or actual homosexual who cannot decide which side of the fence he should be on.

There are of course many instances of cross-identification in which homosexuality does not develop but where the effects are sufficiently damaging to self-identity to be quite noticeable. The cases of Dave and Jerry that we cited earlier are clear examples of this type of effect. Jerry, for example, was an only child whose father died when Jerry was only one year old. He was then raised by his over-possessive, dominant mother and an equally dominant grandmother, so that throughout all the years of his childhood and adolescence his constant companions were two older women. Significantly, throughout his adolescence Jerry never dated any girls, and during his four years in the Marines he showed very little interest in feminine companionship. There was almost no history of sexual exploration of any kind.

Like all young men, Jerry felt that he should get married and have a family, and he finally found a girl in whom he could invest enough affection to risk marriage. He was never able to gratify his wife adequately, but he was able to complete the sex act for a period of time. After a while, the natural fear and repugnance toward women rose to the surface to suppress his sexual drive and he became physically impotent. In this case, as you can see, the cross-identification was based on the almost total absence of the father or any other male figure, and thus the only identification available to him was that with the possessive mother. When Jerry finally understood the relationship between himself and his mother, and why he was deeply afraid of sex relationships and repelled by them, he regained his sexual potency and the marriage relationship was resumed on a more secure basis.

The case of Dave is somewhat different and illustrates

another reason for the failure to achieve self-identity. Dave's father was a hard-driving, self-made, and successful business man who found little time for companionship with his family. In his early years Dave tried desperately to develop secure relationships with his father, but without success. Bitterly disappointed at this rejection, he developed the mechanism of negative identification, by which he resolved unconsciously to be the direct opposite of his father in all things. At the same time, due to the agony of feeling unwanted, he turned to his mother for whatever identification she could provide.

Throughout adolescence the conflict between Dave and his father continued, but mostly at the unconscious level. He wanted desperately to be like his father, whom he actually admired a great deal; but the hatred of his father for rejecting him prevented this wish from developing. While the closeness to his mother provided a feeling of security, he resented and feared the relationship, and sometimes secretly wished his mother were dead. This endless conflict, ambivalence, and cross-identification made it impossible for Dave to achieve any real sex-identity, and as a result he found himself on the threshold of adulthood without any clear idea of what he should be or what he should become. The anarchy of feeling generated by Dave's twisted psychic development had robbed him of his self-identity, and it made impossible the freedom of choice which only the dominion of the intellect can insure. It will take many months of counseling to free this unhappy youngster from the morass of feeling.

Self-identity, as you can see, is a very complex affair. It is in some respects a delicate flower that quickly withers away when its roots are embedded in the soil of inadequate development or unwholesome personal relationships. If the soil is right, it can be nourished into a healthy, robust plant by other experiences and relationships that will help to secure its foundations. Self-identity can be nourished by identification with one's family, by church membership, by loyalty to one's school, or by participating in community activities. Each one of these identifications can act to nourish and support the central, basic conviction of self-identity but, contrariwise, without this central identification of self, all other identifications become pale and meaningless. Lacking self-identity, a person feels alone and confused in a world of meaningless relationships. The faulty image of oneself pays strict homage to the anarchy of one's feelings. You may recall Polonius' advice to Laertes: "This above all: to thine own self be true, and it must follow as the night the day, thou canst not then be false to any man."

8 THE CULT OF INFERIORITY

And the second is like unto it, thou shalt love thy neighbor as thyself.

—MATTHEW 22:37–39.

HAVE YOU EVER NOTICED how often people insist on parading their inferiorities? You would think, wouldn't you, that they would shrink from exposing personal weaknesses and short-comings to the frank and sometimes harshly critical judgments of their friends and colleagues? But no. On the contrary, they seem at times to revel in their lack of knowledge, their physical weaknesses, their sloppy appearance, or even their moral debauchery.

How often we hear people say, "I never could spell very well," "I don't know a thing about geography," "I never was much of a student in college," "I haven't got the brains that the rest of the family has," "Boy, am I getting fat," "I don't know a thing about classical music," "I am a real lush when it comes to women," "I am a weakling where desserts are concerned"—and so on and on through a tiresome litany of self-exposures of human weaknesses and faults that other people are understandably ashamed of. These demeaning self-revelations are what we had in mind when we decided to call this chapter "The Cult of Inferiority." John Steinbeck expressed this attitude precisely when he said, "Most people do not like themselves at all. They distrust themselves, put on masks and pomposities. They quarrel and boast and pretend and are jealous because they do not like themselves. . . . If we could learn to like ourselves even a little, maybe our cruelties and angers might melt away. Maybe we would not have to hurt one another just to keep our ego chins above water."*

Don't think for a moment that these expressions of mediocrity and inferiority bear witness to the virtues of modesty or humility. Quite the contrary. Actually, they are the inadequate person's perverse way of touting his *superiority*. As we shall see more fully later in this chapter, human feelings—especially those that are buried deep in the unconscious—have a way of expressing themselves in qualities or characteristics that are directly opposite to the feeling itself. We have already seen that the unguilty person often feels the most guilty; that the disorder in a person's mind is expressed objectively in a passion for order; and thus inferiority will, more often than not, masquerade as superiority or egotism. So reliable is this proposition that a diagnosis of inferiority can be made without fear of error whenever the attitude of superiority or egocentrism is a part of the individual's psychological armor. When, therefore, he boasts of his lack of knowledge, or his inability to appreciate good music, and so on, he really wants you to think that he is outstanding—even if he has to exploit his own weaknesses to get the point across!

This peculiar tendency of the feeling of inferiority to generate an attitude of superiority is exemplified in a thousand ways in people around us, in famous people who crowd the pages of history, and in innumerable clients who seek the counselor's help in solving their problems. Is there any one of us who hasn't met that most insufferable of all bores—the

* *Words To Live By*, ed. by William L. Nichols (New York, Simon and Schuster, 1959), p. 11. Copyright by Simon and Schuster, Inc.

name-dropper? "B.J. called me into his office to tell me that he was thinking of promoting me to general manager." "Jack called me this morning, but I told him I was too tied up to take a government post at the present time." Familiar? I think so. Familiar, too, are the numerous instances of historical figures whose superiority was undoubtedly spawned by, or in some way related to, inferiority. Teddy Roosevelt, the rugged hero of San Juan Hill, was a physical weakling in his youth. His cousin, F.D.R., attained the greatest political heights despite the severest physical handicap. Or perhaps we should say because of it. Paul, the saint, emerged from a life of sinfulness. Hitler, the most glaring example of paranoid superiority, was a dismal failure as a soldier and artist. Demosthenes, one of the world's greatest orators, had a speech defect. Beethoven was partly deaf; Poe was an alcoholic; Byron had a club foot; the Kaiser of Germany had a withered arm; Napoleon was unbearably short in stature; and that dynamo of energy, John F. Kennedy, has a long history of physical illness.

An imposing list, isn't it? And we could go on like this for many pages more, citing additional instances from real life as well as from counseling experience of the close tie-up between inferiority and superiority. This relationship is so common, and appears clinically with such unvarying regularity, that one cannot avoid the conclusion that there is a cause-effect connection between these two human characteristics. This is exactly what led the renowned Viennese psychiatrist, Alfred Adler, to develop his famous theory of inferiority. As Adler saw it, Nature tends to obscure its weaknesses or failures by the "mechanism" of compensation; and what better way to mask inferiority than by becoming superior, or at least adopting an attitude of superiority? Adler's further theoretical development, leading to the concepts of the "drive for power" and the "masculine protest," is merely an extension of the basic theory of inferiority.

To put these phrases into more common terminology, what Adler was saying is that power (position, status, superiority, wealth, prestige) becomes a psychological necessity in order to offset the damage created by the feeling of inferiority. The masculine protest is an expression of the need to be a man, because man (as compared with woman or child) has the strength, the power, and the status necessary to deal with life and with inferiority. It was the fact that inferiority appeared with such unbroken regularity in his patients that led Adler to the formulation of his theory.

Let us hasten to clarify an aspect of this relationship that may be puzzling. You know, certainly, that there is a great difference between the "name-dropper" and outstanding achievers, like the Roosevelts, Beethoven, or John Kennedy. Both groups express superiority, but in a very different way. And the difference is not at all hard to understand. In the one case there is an *attitude of superiority* with little else to go with it. In the other, there is actually *superior achievement*, and often a superior personality. Yet both are related to, and often grow out of, a sense of inferiority.

The difference is due to the nature of the inferiority itself. Where there exists a strong *feeling* of inferiority, the psychic development is very likely to result in an attitude of superiority. This sort of development gives us the name-dropper, the braggart, the pushy individual, and the conversation hog; and it is especially likely to happen when the feeling of inferiority is unconscious. This we would expect since unconscious feelings are unknown to the person himself, and therefore beyond his control. Because he feels deeply inferior, he is not likely to become an achiever, and thus substitutes the attitude of superiority for superior accomplishment.

Such behavior stands in sharp contrast to that of the person who has achieved superiority in one field or another, and who therefore does not have to "blow his own horn" by such devices as name-dropping or braggadocio. This fact is exemplified with striking clarity in some of the great men of the world and of history. Despite a background of inferiority in many instances, their achievements and their successes stand out so sharply that there is no need for so childish and immature a defense as the attitude of superiority. True greatness, therefore, always walks hand in hand with humility, for the truly superior person knows better than anyone his own weaknesses and limitations, and that the talents which made his achievement possible are the free gift of God.

Why, then, emphasize the fact that many outstanding men were at one time physically inferior? And what about men like Hitler and Napoleon, both of whom were certainly paranoid, and represented the attitude of superiority in its most highly developed and most dangerous form? Even those men whom we would not class with Hitler or Napoleon often show evidence of this taint. Certainly, there are many who would argue strongly that Franklin Roosevelt leaned noticeably in that direction; and that there was a bombast about Theodore Roosevelt that created strong suspicions of an attitude of superiority.

These are fair questions and they demand careful consideration. You realize, of course, that *actual* superiority (in achievement, power, etc.) is often coupled with the *attitude* of superiority. Moreover, history and common observation attest to the fact that many outstanding leaders have been as paranoid as they could be. In our own generation, there are such outstanding examples as Khrushchev, Stalin, Castro, Mussolini, and Hirohito—all of whom reflected strong paranoid trends in their personality. And all of them are excellent examples of how the anarchy of feeling can work toward the degradation if not the destruction of humanity.

Undoubtedly, these men are, or were, capable of superior achievement, and thus became outstanding leaders, but they also lend support to the proposition that the attitude of superiority has its roots in inferiority. Indeed, much of their sadistic destructiveness is traceable to this fact. If Hitler had not felt inferior to the Jews, he would not have had to destroy so many of them. And if Japan, in the person of Hirohito, had not felt so deeply inferior to the United States, it would never have launched its attack on Pearl Harbor. Inferiority, like so many human feelings, is intolerable, and thus ineluctably generates those attitudes and behaviors that will mask or destroy this feeling. And there is nothing so destructive of inferiority as superiority.

But this is so only when inferiority cannot be tolerated and is pushed into the unconscious. In other instances, where inferiority is quite obvious and consciously assimilated to the personality, the reverse often happens, with the result that the person involved actually achieves superiority in his chosen field, and even in other collateral fields. Churchill is not only a great statesman, but also a great writer; but he certainly was an inferior college student. Kennedy is not only outstanding in politics, but he was also an outstanding Naval Officer, and has written a best-selling, Pulitzer Prize biography. In other words, despite the existence of weaknesses, limitations, or inferiority, and spurred on by the desire to eliminate or to overcome inferiority, some persons achieve notable success and outstanding superiority in the very areas of achievement that were most severely limited for them by inferiority. Thus Glenn Cunningham became the world's fastest runner despite the fact that his legs had been burned so severely that it was thought he would never walk again; and Demosthenes became a great orator despite the fact that he had a speech handicap. And who would have guessed that the weak, sickly Theodore Roosevelt would, as he grew older, become a tower of physical strength and endurance?

In emphasizing the role of physical weakness or inferiority in the development of superiority, we do not want to leave the impression that all feelings of inferiority are determined by physical constitution or that superiority is the inevitable outcome of such feelings. Far from it. The crippling sense of inferiority so clearly reflected in the attitudes and behavior of countless persons is generated by a host of factors, some of which are within the person himself and others are a part of his environment or his relationships with other people. If, for example, a parent constantly nags a child to get better grades, criticizes his best efforts, or compares him unfavorably with an older brother, then certainly inferiority is likely to develop. Obviously, this situation would have nothing to do with physical constitution. Similarly, if an Italian boy grows up in a neighborhood which regards Italians as second-class citizens, and is constantly reminded of his "racial inferiority" by the jeers, taunts, and rejections of his peer group, the feeling of inferiority is quite likely to develop.

I am reminded here of a student who had a great deal of difficulty in developing and maintaining healthy interpersonal relationships. He was a tall, well-built, good-looking youngster, about twenty years of age at the time, and a junior in college. He was intelligent and talented, and on initial contact created a good impression. But his social success stopped at this point and never went beyond the first impression. Typically, he had a very high opinion of himself and a very low opinion of others. He was not only the best-looking young man in his group, but he was also the best student, the most talented, and the most sought after by the girls.

"I don't know what's the matter with me, Doc. I know I am better-looking than most of the fellows around here, and that I make a terrific impression when I meet someone for the first time. But somehow the impression doesn't seem to last, and I find that I have very few real friends. Even the girls with whom I am successful in the beginning tend to lose interest in me very quickly. I can't understand it. I know I am smarter than most fellows, and that if I put my mind to it, I could get better grades than the majority of them. I am more talented too. And yet, somehow, I don't seem to be able to make friends very easily. Sometimes I am very lonesome."

This simple story of a young man's anguish in not finding his niche in the social world illustrates a number of points regarding the nature and outcome of inferiority. First of all, we can see very easily how quickly and how firmly superiority becomes imbedded in this type of personality. It also indicates the distortion that can occur under the influence of such feelings. Despite the fact that his interpersonal relationships were very poor, and his actual performance in the academic setting was equally poor, he regarded himself as eminently superior to his fellows.

This is a good clinical instance of the use of superiority to mask a deep, unconscious inferiority. It illustrates the way in which the anarchy of feeling, regardless of the particular feeling involved, tends toward the distortion of judgment about one's self as well as others, undermines a healthy relationship to reality, and interferes with adequate interpersonal relationships. Moreover, in each instance of deep, unconscious feeling (whether of anxiety, inferiority, guilt, or hostility) there is created a pervasive sensitivity that adds its own complications to the behavioral picture. The over-sensitive person—especially one who feels inferior—is acutely vulnerable to all the "slings and arrows of outrageous fortune," and thus is easily and repeatedly hurt by comments, implications, innuendoes, and criticisms.

This hurt will occur even when the "offending" party had no intention whatever of finding fault or criticizing the other person's behavior or appearance. Thus, to say to such a person, "I cannot agree with your opinion," or "You don't look as good in brown as you do in black," is to risk the charge of being hostile or insulting. Objective opinion is twisted into subjective assault. This is the basic, dynamic reason why inferiority is often linked with hostility. The over-sensitive person gets angry very easily, and uses his anger (or hostility) to ward off the implications of inferiority.

Going back for a moment to our college student who felt himself to be so superior to his classmates and chums, we find that his superiority was anchored in an ethnic or social inferiority. Physically he was attractive and well developed, but he had the misfortune of belonging to an ethnic group that was completely rejected by the people in the neighborhood where he lived. As a result, he began to feel socially inferior, and this inferiority spread to other aspects of his personality. In order, therefore, to defend himself from this damaging sense of inferiority, he developed a supremely superior attitude which elevated him to a position far above that of the people who had so harshly rejected him.

We should note here that racial or ethnic inferiority is one of the most common forms of inferiority and has caused more interracial conflict, hatred, and violence than any other single determinant of mass behavior. The Jews, the Negroes, the Catholics, the Southerners, the Japanese, the Italian immigrants, the Cubans—and numerous other minority groups— all suffer from this psychosocial disease. And the credo of all of them is the same: "We want equality," by which they mean, of course, superiority. By the same rule, the incessant demand of the "weaker" sex for equality, recognition, emancipation, freedom, and status has its roots in the same disease of psychosocial inferiority. Significantly, in our culture especially, women have achieved superior roles in many instances. It is not mere colloquialism when some wives are referred to as "the real boss," or as one who "wears the pants" in the family. For a fuller exposition of this trend, see Chapter Nine on "The Feminine Protest."

Cases similar to the one described are seen by the hundreds in counselors' offices. But in order to get a proper perspective on the problem of inferiority, we must realize that it has many sources—some of which are within the person himself, some of which are derived from experiences and relationships, and some of which seem to be imbedded in the nature of man. All of us in a sense experience in some way the feeling of inferiority because of the simple objective fact that *we are contingent, imperfect beings.* To say that we are contingent means that we are inadequate within ourselves to do battle successfully with all the dangers, threats, problems, conflicts, and frustrations that plague our lives day in and day out. Being contingent, we are forced to depend upon other persons or upon outside forces and agencies to cope with successive events, or even just to stay alive. This state of affairs is particularly characteristic of childhood, and it is during childhood that the seeds of psychic inferiority are most securely planted.

Similarly, our inherent imperfections make us tend toward a deep sense of inferiority. How often we feel helplessly inferior when we strive desperately for distant goals, not realizing, or refusing to admit, that the imperfections within us make the goal practically unattainable. This sense of inferiority is deepened to a painful degree when we see those around us striding relentlessly toward the very goals that we ourselves cannot reach. How inferior we feel when temptation and sinfulness sweep over us like a tidal wave and engulf all of our noble aspirations, ideals, and purposes. And when to this despair is added the crushing sense of guilt, our feeling of inferiority breaks through all boundaries and spreads throughout the entire personality. Small wonder, then, in the face of such widespread imperfection and contingency, that the sense of inferiority has become so general a trait among the races of men.

When this existential inferiority is reinforced by the dependencies and inadequacies of childhood, the inferiority generated by comparison of the sexes, personal failures, the effects of chronic illness and bodily handicaps, the demands imposed by parental perfectionism, racial and ethnic inferiority, and a host of other inferiority-breeding elements in the lives of children, it is surprising that more people are not psychologically crippled. The child is born into a world that is often designed to foster weakness and dependency, and thus to encourage the feeling of inferiority. Insurance programs, college-aid programs, social security, workmen's compensation, prolonged dependency of children on parents, financially supported marriages—all tend to foster the cult of inferiority.

While it is natural for the feeling of inferiority to generate an attitude of superiority, especially when it is deep within the personality structure and exerts a damaging effect, there are other ways in which it expresses itself in personality characteristics and behavior. Like guilt and hostility, it can show its face directly, or it can hide behind a mask that appears as its direct opposite. When inferiority works its way into attitudes and behavior without benefit of masking, the personality is then characterized by extreme shyness, hesitancy, indecision, timidity, and social anxiety. Such a person always begins an expression of opinion with some qualifying phrase. He cannot say directly and bluntly, "I think that . . ."; but he must preface his opinion with, "I may be wrong, but . . . ," or "My opinion isn't worth much, but. . . ." Or, what is very common is to sit quietly in the group and never venture an opinion at all.

In order to understand the personality controlled by inferiority, we must grasp the essential fact that inferiority is basically social in nature, and derives in part from odious comparisons of one's self with other persons in the environment, or with values and standards that have been imposed by some authority figure. Inferiority always implies a *subordinate* position or status, one that is not as good as that of others. You must remember, too, that this might come about by self-imposed, perfectionistic standards that a person builds for himself or acquires from his surroundings. In such cases he feels inferior because he repeatedly fails to measure up to the image or ideal he has created for himself. This sort of thing is likely to happen if some idealized person in the environment, such as a mother or father, possesses outstanding and superior characteristics and achievements. Typically, in his striving to emulate this ideal, the child may often fail miserably, with feelings of inferiority an almost inevitable outcome. If one is that kind of parent, he must be sure not to set standards that are too high for his children, and always take care to encourage them to perform in terms of their capacity rather than his.

Here we might remind ourselves of the close connections between different feelings that we experience. For example, sinfulness or immoral behavior will make you feel guilty, and that itself can cause considerable difficulty. But the very fact of sinfulness is itself a sign of weakness and failure, and therefore it seems to you that you are not as good a person as you could be, and probably, as you see it, much worse than others around you. In other words, where moral behavior is concerned, you might well conclude that you are inferior and as a consequence develop a deep sense of inferiority.

This sort of thing is especially likely to happen to the person who discovers that repeated commitments to moral improvement are really nothing more than a litany of moral failures. Sinfulness and guilt are natural handmaids to the feeling of inferiority. Beware of this moral trap into which we so easily fall. Remember that sinfulness is the common lot of weak and imperfect mankind, and that you cannot expect to be an exception. Where your human shortcomings are concerned, learn to be moral without being moralistic. Learn to distinguish between *being* inferior because you are a human being, and *feeling* inferior because sometimes you fail to live up to high standards.

In much the same way that inferiority is related to guilt, so is it reinforced by a feeling of inadequacy. These three feelings are closely bound to each other because they are all nurtured in the soil of human weakness, incompetence, or failure. Thus, moral failure leads to the feeling of guilt; intellectual failure to the feeling of inadequacy; and both to the feeling of inferiority. But there is a difference between inadequacy and inferiority that must be noted. Inferiority results from, or is encouraged by, comparison of oneself with the abilities and achievements of others. Inadequacy, on the other hand, results from the conviction that, regardless of the qualities or achievements of others, one does not possess necessary or desired attributes.

For example, if you fail to complete a course of studies in college, no matter how hard you try, you may well feel inferior to those who do succeed; but you will also feel inadequate. Obviously, the one feeling tends to reinforce and to compound the other, often producing a crippling sense of incompetency in the face of everyday demands and responsibilities. Typically, the young housewife and mother feels totally inadequate to the task of maintaining a home, managing the budget, or raising her children. In such instances, the feeling of inadequacy produces a sense of helplessness that may end in acute anxiety, extreme nervousness, frustration, or nervous collapse. This we see strikingly illustrated in women who react with severe emotional breakdown after the birth of a child.

The feeling of inadequacy may and often does produce more damage to the personality than inferiority. It is unpleasant to think that we are inferior to our fellow men, and the realization of this may be traumatic; but it is sometimes more traumatic to discover that we do not possess within ourselves the resources that we ought to have to meet our responsibilities. Inadequacy refers more directly to weaknesses in the self than does inferiority. But we must always remember that inadequacy is only a matter of degree, that everyone is inadequate in one way or another, and that the human personality has tremendous resources for growth and for learning.

Imagine the young mother who is at wit's end in her efforts to handle the demands and responsibilities of her first-born child. Yet, a few years later, this same "inadequate" young woman is seen dispatching the affairs of three and four and five children with relative ease and remarkable efficiency. The inadequacy is gone, and so is the feeling that threatened to cripple her a few years before, because she gave the resources within her personality a chance to promote growth and learning and understanding. Don't let responsibilities either fool you or frighten you. Few of them are as big or as threatening as they seem, and most of them we learn quickly to cope with. Don't let the *feeling* of inadequacy push you over the brink into helplessness or anxiety. Remember that human personality —your personality—is the most resourceful instrument ever invented.

Now you can see from this analysis how feelings compound and reinforce each other, and often lead to further difficulties in the psychological realm. Inadequacy, guilt, and inferiority are very likely to breed *insecurity*, and the feeling of insecurity is the most powerful determinant of *anxiety*. To be inadequate or inferior, especially in critical situations, means that when we are supposed to act resolutely and effectively we are shackled by our own weaknesses and shortcomings, and thus unable to cope with the demands or threats of daily life. You can see what this will do. It will make you feel unsure of yourself, exposed to all sorts of threatening elements in your environment, and therefore unsafe. It's like being in a rickety old building when there is a hundred-mile-an-hour wind blowing outside. It is this sort of situation, transferred to the psychological realm, that creates the feeling of insecurity. To feel insecure is to feel unsafe, uncertain within oneself that disaster is not right around the corner. You can see why the feeling of insecurity so quickly breeds that most damaging of all emotional states—anxiety.

At this point we encounter a common phenomenon in the affairs of the mind, and that is *the vicious circle of feelings.*

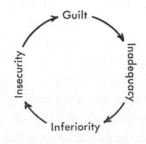

THE VICIOUS CIRCLE OF FEELINGS

Guilt breeds inadequacy and inferiority, which in turn breed insecurity. But the feeling of insecurity will in its turn breed anxiety, which is the forerunner of uncertainty, inadequacy, and insecurity. It's like the old story of the fellow who started worrying because he could not sleep, and could not sleep because of worrying. That's the way it is with the anarchy of feeling: a vicious circle is quickly developed, and the unhappy victim finds it impossible to break into this circle because he cannot find a point at which it begins.

You are aware, of course, that there are a number of side-effects that result from this state. When you feel anxious and insecure, you become less decisive, less willing to pin your hopes and ambitions on decisions that might possibly be wrong. And this of course undermines self-confidence to an alarming degree. A young man recently came to my office to get some help on the choice of a career. Should he go into medicine, as his cousin advises, or should he go into law? If he goes into medicine it means additional years of training, and after all he might find that medicine isn't suited to him. Besides, he might meet a girl and want to get married, and then he could not finish his studies. On the other hand, his cousin, a doctor, agreed to "foot the bill" for his medical education. Besides, medicine would enable him to realize a lifelong ambition of helping other people. But the profession of law also has its attractions. It requires fewer years of training, offers broader opportunities for success, and does not make the same demands that medicine does. And so around and around he goes, deciding one moment for medicine and the next for law. And when he finally left my office he was no closer to a decision than when he came in.

This is a story all too common at the age period that marks the transition from youth to adulthood. Untold numbers of high school seniors and college students are caught in the web of indecision regarding their future roles in the world of business or the professions, and also as husbands and fathers, wives and mothers. Inadequacy and insecurity have a great deal to do with this indecision, but we must recognize that much of it comes from the failure of young people to achieve *self-identity* during the years of adolescence and early adulthood. Not having a clear and precise concept of themselves—a problem that often stems from the failure to achieve sex-identity—they find it difficult to project themselves into future roles.

Many of them don't even know what it is like to be a man or a woman in the full sense of those terms. Thus the typical complaints of the young adult: "I haven't the faintest idea of what I want to be," "I majored in English because I couldn't think of anything else," "Marriage doesn't appeal to me—it involves too many responsibilities," "I just can't see myself in the role of a father," or "There are so many occupations to choose from I don't know where to start." You can see readily enough how this lack of self-identity will act to reinforce insecurity, and thus contribute to an almost pathological indecisiveness. Important and critical decisions can only be made quickly and efficiently by persons whose ego or self is well developed and integrated into a dynamic, forceful unit within the personality.

Here, then, we have the story of inferiority—one of the most important facets of the anarchy of feeling. You have seen what inferiority is like, where it comes from, and how it is bound up with other feelings in the makeup of personality. You have seen also what it does to personality and behavior, and to the person's relationship with others. In some instances it can function as the cornerstone of achievement; but in the majority of cases it leads to a lack of self-confidence, pseudo-superiority, indecisiveness, excessive timidity, and social backwardness. It can and often does lead to negative and damaging personality characteristics, and sets a severe limit on accomplishment. For these reasons, its stranglehold should be broken as quickly and as thoroughly as possible.

As with all such negative feelings, we must first of all come to grips with the existence of inferiority and the part that it is playing in our behavior and our relationships with others. Many persons who have deep feelings of inferiority would be the first to deny it. They mistakenly equate the *feeling* of inferiority with *being* inferior, and thus feel safer or more comfortable by closing their eyes to it. You should take particular note of the fact that persons who squarely confront actual inferiority, such as a serious physical handicap, very often capitalize on this frank awareness by superior achievement. Helen Keller, Franklin Roosevelt, and Glenn Cunningham are striking examples of the success of compensation based upon a sensible, intelligent awareness of personal limitations. It is only when you hide your inferiorities or inadequacies from yourself, and try to hide them from others, that personality damage is likely to result.

You must remember too that inferiority of any kind is only relative and results from foolish and unrealistic comparisons with others. First of all, from a standard of perfection all of us are inferior, and therefore we must learn to accept the inevitability of weaknesses, mistakes, inadequacies, and failures. Secondly, in respect to any particular trait, capacity, or characteristic, all of us would fall at a point somewhere between perfection and gross imperfection or between high level performance and extremely poor performance. For example, if you have an I.Q. of 110, that means that all persons above that point would be superior to you in intelligence, but also that you would be superior to all persons below that point. If you are a good cook, then you are better than mediocre or poor cooks, and subordinate to the experts. If you are good-looking, then you are neither beautiful nor ugly. When we look at the problem of inferiority in this way, we see that it very largely disappears. Since so-called inferiority is purely relative, it turns out that the "inferior" person is in many respects "superior" to many of his fellowmen. Once these facts about the feeling of inferiority are clearly realized and accepted, it can be broken loose from the anarchy of feeling, and the unfortunate victim's personal resources can be freed for more worthwhile accomplishments.

9 THE FEMININE PROTEST

Maids must be wives and mothers to fulfill the entire and holiest end of woman's being.

—FRANCES ANN KEMBLE.

IN ANY POPULAR MAGAZINE, the chances are ten to one that a majority of the ads will center on some aspect of physical womanhood, particularly that symbol of the modern, emancipated woman, the bustline. Nowhere do we find the cult of inferiority developed to a greater extreme; because, underlying this brackish appeal to the love of physical charm and seductiveness, is a message plain for all to see: "Don't be inferior. You too can be alluring, seductive, and sexy. Just wear a Mermaidform Bra."

This tendency in women toward feelings of inferiority has a long history. From the beginning of time, women have been cast in an inferior role in most cultures, and there were some dauntless males who occasionally raised the question whether woman even had a soul. This role-casting, of course, was always firmly in the control of the male of the species, who cleverly exploited this technique for two major purposes: one, to establish his own superiority, and two, to maintain something of a despotic control over the weaker sex.

Let it be noted, however, that women have contributed to maintaining their own inferior status. This they accomplished quite adroitly in at least three different ways. First of all, the majority of them accepted the weak, passive, dependent role that man assigned to them, and thus strengthened the theory spread widely by their male counterparts that women are actually inferior to men. Secondly, whenever occasion permitted, they went even further and exploited the weaknesses supposedly inherent in their nature. They put forth repeated claims to physical weakness and illness, insisted on certain niceties and courtesies which could only be accorded a weaker sex, and took every occasion to embroider the fact of their frailty. Thirdly, they committed the blunder of emphasizing their inferiority by demanding emancipation, freedom, and equality, not only with respect to their male counterparts, but also with respect to their natural roles of mother, wife, housekeeper, and homemaker. If ever there were any doubt of feminine inferiority, women themselves have worked desperately at eliminating it. In other words, they engaged in a huge protest—a protest against being feminine, against the feeling of inferiority, against the roles that nature, God, and man expected them to play. Their most violent protest has been directed at the uterus, and they have connived with all their might at developing instruments and techniques whereby the fertility of the uterus could be sealed off very effectively. As Shakespeare said in another connection, "they protested too much," and thus reinforced the conviction that deep within themselves and in the minds of men they really are inferior.

This protest against femininity, motherhood, and distinctively feminine roles is not enough to define the entire content of "the feminine protest." There is more to it than this, because the term embodies the implication that women have not merely protested against certain conditions and situations, but *they have protested too much*. Many of my readers will undoubtedly recognize the similarity of this phrase, "the feminine protest," to the one used so effectively by Alfred Adler in the development of his theory of inferiority. You will recall that Adler had rounded out his theory by inventing the idea of "the masculine protest," by which he signified the striving within all persons to overcome inferiority by "being a man." Adler argued that everyone was dynamically affected by the masculine protest, because man represents the embodiment of strength, power, virility, and domination, all of which could serve effectively to destroy or at least to placate the feeling of inferiority. And certainly there is a great deal of evidence in the behavior of untold numbers of people to support Adler's theory. The almost universal lust for power, for status, for prestige, for wealth, and a host of other qualities and characteristics that bespeak superiority, indicates quite clearly that Adler had discovered an important facet of the human mind. But it is equally clear that this powerful need to establish the fact (or maybe the illusion) of manhood, masculinity, or power is overwhelming testimony to the existence of inferiority. It is a clinically established fact that the *attitude* of superiority (as distinct from the *fact* of superiority) is always dynamically determined by the feeling or the conviction of inferiority.

You can see of course the close parallel at this point between the ideas of the masculine and the feminine protest. While we will explain in more detail just what the feminine protest is, and what it signifies for the psychic makeup of modern woman, it is clear that both mechanisms have their roots in inferiority. And this fact betrays one of the strangest paradoxes in the whole history of woman's struggle to break through the chains of enslavement and to walk the earth with the same freedom as her sexual counterpart. For woman, in striving to be free, equal, and emancipated, *has lost her free-*

dom to be herself. In her passionate desire for emancipation from the shackles of the kitchen and the nursery, she created an image of woman that at best is a caricature of nature. In loosening the bonds that tied her to the home, she has become ensnarled in the tentacles of the typewriter, the subway, and the file cabinet. Whether she knows it or not, woman's so-called freedom today is a caricature of real freedom, since in emancipating her personality she has lost her soul. There can be no freedom apart from self-realization; and the woman of today has lost the secret of how to actualize herself. In creating and fulfilling the image of the free, unfettered woman, she forgot how important it is to strive for an ideal that is a projection of natural woman. To rescue herself from this unhappy situation, modern woman will have to realize that the image created for the sake of freedom is a caricature that bears only small resemblance to the real thing. In the words of C. A. Stoddard, "There can be no higher ambition for a Christian woman than to be a faithful wife and a happy and influential mother. It is a place which God has given woman, and she who fills it well, is as honorable and honored as the most illustrious man can be."

As distinct from the masculine protest which proclaims in loud tones the desire to be a man and in that way reduces inferiority or a feeling of weakness, the feminine protest proclaims in equally strident tones the intense wish or need to be a woman. Thus has the historical process of defining the nature of womanhood come full circle. The anarchic feelings of weakness, helplessness, inequality, and inferiority which provided the power to achieve political suffrage, to crack open the world of business and of politics, and to escape from the tyranny of the uterus, are the same feelings that now motivate the feminine protest, which in simple terms is the need to prove to the world that after all modern woman is really feminine. The powerful need to be equal to and identical with the male has wrought a deep anxiety in the soul of modern woman because she realizes unconsciously that she has lost her own identity, and the loss of identity will invariably lead to neurotic anxiety or to panic. When this happens there is a frantic effort to recapture the lost identity, and in women this emerges as the feminine protest. In Adlerian language, this protest is an overt compensation for deep feelings of inferiority and lack of identity. Thomas à Kempis expressed the same idea in another way: "We should have much peace if we would not busy ourselves with the sayings and doings of others."

This feminine protest is expressed in many different ways, but perhaps most strikingly in the widespread emphasis among women on typical feminine characteristics. While many women do nothing whatever to emphasize either the mass or the form of their breasts, the success of advertisements which stress the importance of certain bodily contours is testimony to the widespread effort of women to exploit this physical quality in the interest of establishing their own femininity. And those who offend most flagrantly in this regard are often childless, thrice married, or involved in some sordid affair in which *physical* femininity plays a leading role. The "sweater girl" of thirty years ago is a striking example of this type of frantic femininity. It is worth noting in this connection the inverse relationship between the natural, nutritive function of the female breast and its unnatural use as a sex symbol that serves the purpose of the feminine protest. The more that women gave up breast-feeding their children and relinquished this function in favor of the bottle, the more they exploited this part of the human anatomy for sexual purposes.

In days gone by a woman could nurse her child at the breast without shame. Nowadays the breast has become an object of shameful nudity. One is tempted to believe that the guilt which many women have experienced because of their abandonment of the natural function of the breast is the basic, unconscious reason why so many women have turned to emphasizing its sexual possibilities. The reasoning is simple. The breast must have some function, and since it no longer has a nutritive one, then the only thing to do is to invest it with a sexual function.

This undue emphasis on certain physical contours of the feminine body has many parallels, but none of them have the same significance for the dynamics of the feminine protest that this emphasis has. We know of the endless and almost compulsive efforts to maintain or to restore the alluring feminine form by diets, exercises, corsets and girdles. We know, too, that the leg is made more shapely by excessively high heels, and that other feminine characteristics or contours can be emphasized in certain ways to serve the interests of the feminine protest. If nothing else, there is always the revealing bathing suit to establish the incontrovertible fact of femininity, and this dynamic reaches its greatest influence in the bikini. How can one doubt the existence of femininity in the face of such striking evidence?

But the effort to establish femininity is not limited to these more obvious signs of feminine protest. The tight-fitting dress permits a certain amount of seduction without guilt. Note the startling hairdos, the exotic perfumes, and the vari-colored hose that women of today wear. Note also the lengthy fingernails that range in color from a baby pink to a deep black. And then there is the garish use of lipstick in order to make the mouth more alluring, the eye-shadow, the tailored eyebrows, the tinkling earrings, the jewelry, the furs, and many other jimcracks and gadgets that support the unconscious assertion, "I am a woman."

The significant fact that relates all this unquestionably to the feminine protest is that none of these trappings is necessary to establish the fact of femininity. Indeed, they have little to do with femininity as such. They are no more expressive of true femininity than the padded shoulders of men's jackets, a mustache, or a deep voice are signs of masculinity in the male. As is always true, where inferiority or lack of self-identity is the motivating factor, the more embellishments become necessary, the more certain it is that the characteristic they supposedly demonstrate does not actually exist. The name-dropper, who attempts to establish his superiority by identification with important people, clearly betrays his own inferiority, and the more he name-drops, boasts of his accomplishments, and protests his own superiority, the more certain it is that he has no superiority.

We are not suggesting that these trappings of masculinity or femininity are unconsciously determined in every instance by the feeling of inferiority or the need to establish sex identity. We are well aware that many of these embellishments are consciously—and quite normally—used to enhance the quality of sexual allure. But it must be obvious that the more necessary a woman feels these extrinsic embellishments to be for exploiting her femininity, the more she betrays uncertainty about her sex status. And this is clearly exemplified in countless modern women who substitute the externals of femininity for a truly feminine role out of the lack of any deep conviction that they are truly feminine. This is the essential dynamic of the feminine protest—the urgent need to assert the fact of femininity in the face of a deep underlying conviction that somehow feminine identity has been lost.

In the clinic and in the counseling room, it is not at all uncommon to meet the most attractive, well-dressed, stylishly coiffured, and even seductive women who, at the age of thirty, or thirty-five, or forty, remain unattached, unloved, and in a strange way unattractive. These are not career women who have abandoned all thoughts of marriage, children, and a home because of the demands of their chosen work. Nor are they women who have dedicated their lives to a particular cause for which the single state would be a great advantage. And certainly, by any standards, they are not women lacking in physical attractiveness. But they are all alike in one particular respect—they lack the essential spark of femininity. They do not possess a clearly defined sex identity, nor have they identified themselves with typical feminine roles.

For example, there is the case of a lovely, attractive young woman, twenty-nine years of age, who on three successive occasions has become engaged, set the date for marriage, made all the necessary arrangements, and then called it off at the last minute. She wanted desperately to be like other girls, and she possessed all of the physical qualities that any man would be proud of in a wife. And yet this charming young woman could not do what was necessary to establish a lasting marital relationship, and that was to project herself into the roles of wife and mother. She was lacking in sex identity; she did not clearly conceive of herself as a woman, and felt somewhat uncomfortable in relationships with men. Characteristically, she used all of the gadgets to prove that she was essentially and deeply feminine, but deep within the recesses of her personality was the conviction that she lacked femininity, and could not therefore fulfill the roles of wife and mother that every woman is supposed to fulfill, or at least to be able to fulfill.

What of those women who, having forsaken natural feminine roles, are content to compete with men in the marketplace, in the classroom, or in the consulting room? Are they, too, expressions of the feminine protest? And what of those women who affect men's attire, dress in the most casual and unladylike fashion, who drink their men friends under the table, compete with them in the sports arena, or boast openly that they are more at home in the company of men than of women? Are they, in some strange manner, also examples of the feminine protest?

To answer these questions, we must first recognize that these two types of modern woman—the one who overemphasizes femininity and the other who denies it—have a common breeding ground. They both represent most clearly the influence of inferiority and inequality; both are victims of the failure of sex-identity; and both are protesting in their own way against the role of women in our society. Both also betray the feeling that somehow true femininity has been lost or weakened, or that femininity should be deserted in favor of masculine characteristics that are stronger and more secure.

The motivation, therefore, is essentially the same in both instances. But the one has abandoned the fight to achieve femininity and has adopted the masculine protest as a means of solving the problem of identity. This caricature of womanhood no longer believes in the essential worth of femininity and has cast her lot with the male of the species. She defiantly enters the arena of male competition and achievement with the bold assertion, "What a man can do, I can do, and perhaps even better." She is often the medical specialist, the researcher, the real estate operator, or the hardheaded psychiatrist. On weekends she is often seen attired in mannish clothes, a drink in one hand and a cigarette in the other, chatting amiably with a group of men about the vagaries of the stock market, the breeding of horses, or the stupidity of women who devote their lives to the raising of children. We have said that she is a caricature of womanhood. Perhaps it would be more correct to say that she is the complete negation of femininity, a creature who has lost her soul because her protest against her natural role has carried her beyond the feminine protest into the doubtful security of the masculine protest.

The other type of woman whose femininity escapes her because of inferiority and lack of self-identity is engaged in a last-ditch effort to reclaim femininity from the abyss of her own negations. She does not ally herself with the role of the male, but instead attempts to re-establish femininity by the process of over-compensation. Femininity to her is a priceless jewel which she causes to sparkle by all of the trappings of external femininity. But she does not know that femininity cannot be purchased simply by physical allure, stylish clothing, or the embellishments of the beauty shop. She does not realize that femininity is a deeply biological and psychological quality that involves a commitment to the age-old and undeniable role of being a full-time wife and mother.

Deep within herself, in the hidden recesses of her unconscious psyche, she realizes that femininity has become unhinged, that it no longer has a secure anchor in her being, but has become weakened and attenuated. Knowing this, and wanting desperately not to admit it to herself, she strikes out in a desperate effort to prove to herself and to the world that her unconscious is lying to her. She moves in the direction, not of masculinity, but of the feminine protest, so that all may see how truly feminine she is despite the fact that she is childless, incapable of motherhood, and devoid of the ability to attract or to hold a man for more than a short period of time. Her protest is voiced with greater anguish than that of the "masculine" woman, because she knows unconsciously what has happened to her innermost self. Here again the anarchy of feeling is seen in one of its most vivid forms, for there is no greater anarchy than that of depriving a person of his own identity.

What is it that lies behind this peculiar denial and affirmation of femininity? Is it just an historical sequence of inferiority, emancipation, equality, and loss of identity? These are certainly the essential ingredients of the feminine protest as it finally emerged in modern woman; but there are certain aspects of this development that need some elaboration. It must be granted that there are countless women in different lands who have not become victimized by inferiority and the lure of equality, and consequently have not lost their sense of personal identity. But the number who have is increasing daily, and the impact of this feminine development is being felt in many ways. For this reason we should probe as deeply as we can into the causes of this phenomenon.

Let us look at the question of feminine inferiority and see if we can't get at the truth regarding the relative position of the two sexes. It is undeniable, of course, that the two sexes are deeply different, not only in their physical and morphologic characteristics, but also and more significantly in their psychic constitution. Women feel differently and therefore think differently than men, and they want different things, and on their own terms. Women, for example, have a stronger need to love and to be loved; they need to cherish and to be cherished more strongly than do men; they need more deeply to find their identity and their personal worth in another person or persons rather than in a job, a crusade, or a research project. The fact that some women find their identity in things other than persons only means that they have capitulated to the masculine protest. To argue, as some do, that women are equal to men and therefore possess the same potentialities or needs is to yield to the most prejudiced type of thinking.

One must also recall the significant biological fact that women are ordained to pregnancy, and therefore to the raising of a family. In this quality they are fundamentally different from the male, and no amount of social or economic equality, and no style of dress or change in manners, can alter this fact. There are also the deeply significant facts of the menstrual cycle and the menopause, the first of which has been most aptly described as the tyranny of the moon. Both of these characteristics are essential parts of feminine physiology and psychology, and are intimately related to the problem of inferiority and the feminine protest.

These three biological qualities reflect fundamental differences between the two sexes, and these differences are often the starting point of inferiority. For many women both menstruation and pregnancy are abominations, and later on in life they will regard the menopause in the same way; and these women look enviously at the carefree male who is not burdened with these "inferior" limitations. It is this attitude towards intrinsic feminine characteristics that leads to the denial of identity and the gradual evolution of the feminine protest. And this denial of essential femininity has left modern woman without spiritual roots, and with no more spiritual nourishment than that provided by a vacuous equality and independence.

If, therefore, by inferiority is meant physical smallness or relative weakness, or that women are by nature committed to the tyranny of the uterus or of the moon, then feminine inferiority certainly exists. But the one is unimportant, and the other a myth created by over-zealous feminists who fostered the tragic delusion that independence and equality are adequate substitutes for intrinsic femininity. Moreover, it is often pointed out that the inferiority of women is also reflected in a much poorer record of achievement. In the arts and sciences, in politics and business, in philosophy and theology women have failed to record any appreciable achievements; and out of this charge has come a frantic scramble for achievement, recognition, and status. "Anything that men can do, we can do, and perhaps even better" is the battle cry of those women stung by the whiplash of inferiority. What a foolish and hopeless ambition! Foolish because it is based upon a hope for reversal of roles, and hopeless because in the economy of nature it can never be realized. Since man first crawled out of the slime of the sea, there has been a necessary division of labor, for the simple reason that the sexes are both different and complementary. For women to attempt to match masculine achievement makes about as much sense as a man yearning for impregnation so that he too can boast of having a child.

It is not at all a question of whether women have the capabilities to achieve great things in the world of science and letters, but only of whether the economy of nature would permit them to do so. There is no evidence to show that women are intellectually inferior to men; but there is ample evidence to demonstrate conclusively that the talents of the feminine mind can be utilized more effectively in some situations than in others. Moreover, women have demonstrated clearly in recent years that they are quite capable of performing many jobs successfully, and of worthwhile achievements that match many of which men like to boast. Thus the insensate striving for equality has become something of an anachronism.

But even more important is the fact that the criteria of achievement are often poorly defined or misapplied, not to mention the fact that most of them have been devised by men to measure their own accomplishments. It is certainly marvelous to build an empire, formulate a philosophical system, or invent a new schema of mathematical symbols. But who would say that any one of these accomplishments outstrips in importance or in greatness the building of a good home or the rearing of a healthy, right-minded family? It is the children of such families who are destined to take over all of the tomorrows regardless of empires or philosophical systems. When the genius of a good wife and mother is applied successfully in this direction, the fruits are often far greater in social significance than all the vaunted achievements of men.

It is unfortunate that so little attention and merit have been given to this important and noble achievement of which woman alone is capable. It is true that each year we observe Mother's Day, or even select a Mother of the Year. We mark these occasions in somewhat trite fashion, and then wait for another year to roll around before we again pay homage to this achievement. But nowhere is her name inscribed in marble or even in the pages of *Who's Who* to proclaim to the world that here is an achievement that the highest genius of man cannot surpass.

Equally unfortunate are those habits of mind and of tradition that serve to foster the spurious inferiority of the "weaker" sex. In many different ways the supposed inferiority of women is emphasized in attitudes, in proscriptions, and in various limitations imposed in the area of work, play, and social relations. In women the natural, *ontological* inadequacy of human nature is reinforced by a *feeling* of inferiority engendered by ignorance and superstition. We all feel this inadequacy and inferiority of our nature, and we instinctively rebel against it. You can well imagine what happens when to this natural inadequacy is added the inferiority of sexual status, of exclusion from different activities, or of failure of achievement. This anarchic feeling becomes almost intolerable, and will invariably generate behavior or attitudes designed to offset it. This is what we see in modern woman's attempt to emulate, or to identify with, masculinity, and also in the feminine protest whereby she boldly reasserts her basic femininity.

What are the consequences of woman's inadequate perception of herself, and of her role in the general scheme of things? And what can she do about it? There are at least three damaging effects that can result from woman's attitude toward herself—role diffusion, loss of identity, and a deep conflict within her being that often leads to serious disruptions within her psychic structure. Many women today are expected to play, or insist on playing, too many roles, so that their selfhood becomes diffused among many diverse activities. At one time, not too long ago, the woman was expected to be a wife and mother, and her role was clearly defined and circumscribed by whatever responsibilities and privileges these concepts involved. Nowadays she is often expected to be a wife and mother, office worker, executive, or teacher, chauffeur for the children or the commuting husband, hostess and travelling companion, and whatever else the husband cannot fit into his own busy schedule. This role diffusion dissipates the ego, and robs it of the strength it needs to fulfill its responsibilities of coping with the multifarious demands of reality.

Role diffusion is indeed only one step removed from the loss of self-identity, which is the second effect of the feminine protest. But this effect has even wider implications for the mental health and stability of today's woman because it leads to a deep confusion within her psychic being as to what she is, where she fits into the scheme of things, and where she is going. In addition to the numerous advertisements for the frilly trappings of femininity, she is also constantly reminded by newspapers and magazines, by radio and television, of the joys and privileges of having children. Motherhood, against which she has been warned by over-anxious parents, friends, and the Planned Parenthood Association, is nevertheless extolled as a virtue and a lofty ideal. The husband who supposedly loves her, and just as supposedly wants to be the father of her children, is overjoyed when she decides to continue working after marriage; and secretly they connive at sealing off the uterus while keeping the vagina free for "sexual companionship." Now she has attained the ultimate in confusion and loss of identity. She is both wife and provider; cook and housemaid; bed-partner and co-worker. But what is she really supposed to be? How can she be all of these different things and be any of them well? And what happened to the glorious ideal of motherhood? Is it really good to seal off the uterus? Is she really a wife to her husband, or something else? Are the concepts of wife and motherhood really separable? What am I? What am I supposed to be? These are the questions of the person who has failed to achieve or has lost self-identity. And this psychological quality of self-identity grows out of the essential being of the person. It is the essence of woman to love and to be loved, to cherish and to be cherished, to have children and to raise a family; and when this essential concept is diffused into many different roles, self-identity will certainly be lost.

The third effect of feminine inferiority is closely bound up with the other two—role diffusion and loss of self-identity. This is a deep conflict within the recesses of the female personality that tends to tear it apart, and to generate pervasive neurotic processes and symptoms. This conflict is as much ontological as it is psychological, although it is most clearly manifested in the psychic order. The essence of this type of conflict is expressed in the biblical phrase "No man can serve two masters"; and by the same rule no woman can aspire to womanhood and to something else that contradicts womanhood at the same time.

This attitude is more than a negation of roles; it is a negation of one's being. To substitute the vagina for the uterus as so many modern women do, or deliberately to allow the uterus to remain fallow, is to cause a deep split within the soul of the person. This is the level at which the conflict begins, although eventually it will end in the development of psychological mechanisms and symptoms. Here is one of the reasons why so much psychic pain and guilt are generated by the implications of the menopause. It is then that the conflict comes into full bloom, since it is impossible to escape from the realization that motherhood, so flagrantly and callously tossed aside, is no longer possible. It is then that the full impact of the desertion of femininity is felt, perhaps for the first time. In the early stages of womanhood, it is relatively easy to rationalize choices and behaviors that are fundamentally contrary to natural impulses and needs. But no amount of rationalization can obscure the implications of the menopause.

The results of this realization are various and depend upon a number of conditions and characteristics. In some instances there is a great deal of guilt, self-accusation, and depression, setting the stage for the disorder recognized as involutional melancholia. In others, there is a frantic effort to compensate for the failure to achieve full womanhood by excessive dieting in order to retain a youthful figure; by youthful styling of hair, socializing with young people, learning to dance in the style of youth, and wearing clothes that are very similar to those worn by teenagers. In this type of behavior we see another expression of the feminine protest. It is as though women are trying to say: "I haven't been much of a mother, but as you can see, I am every inch a woman."

This pathetic effort to recapture lost femininity is no longer determined so much by inferiority as by the feelings of guilt, and the failure of adequate identity. This is why excessive drinking, sleeplessness, and other disabling neurotic symptoms are often the constant companion of women whose lives have lost their meaning. It is also the reason why, in a last desperate effort to reclaim femininity, many otherwise virtuous wives become involved in flirtations and affairs that will prove to them, and maybe even to others, that the precious gift of femininity is not altogether lost.

If this picture appears bleak, and possibly over-drawn, we must remember that it is only part of the story of the growing disablement caused by psychological impairment, which often has its roots in the anarchy of feeling. We are quite aware that it would be impossible to reverse the trend toward feminine emancipation from the kitchen and nursery, that young women will enter the marketplace at least until the marriage bonds are securely tied, and that the number of working mothers will probably continue to increase. As one outstanding feminist put it recently, we cannot go back to the time when women found their fulfillment in the home. But this somewhat discouraging prediction does not alter the fact that countless women are the victims of inferiority, lack of self-identity, and the feminine protest. Whether they give up their jobs and learn to embrace the career of motherhood or not, the fact remains that they will not disengage themselves from the feminine protest, escape the ravages of neurotic illness, or avoid the disabling depressions of the menopause until they rediscover their own identity. They must abandon the myth of equality with men, and they must learn to avoid the pitfalls of inferiority. Only by asserting their own personal worth as women, and reasserting as vigorously as possible their own identity, can these women ever hope to reclaim femininity. Without these assertions, they can expect to be bogged down forever in the quicksand of the feminine protest.

10 THE LOGIC OF ANARCHY

The wish, Harry, is father to the thought.

—SHAKESPEARE.

"I HATE HIM," exclaimed the young man in referring to the uncle who had given him a home and an education since the death of his parents in a fatal automobile crash. "I hate him. And I am glad I hate him, because if I didn't—well, I might get to like him, and I know that he likes me. And I wouldn't like that because I hate him!"

Here, in the starkest kind of neurotic realism, is exemplified the peculiar logic of emotional anarchy. In it we see the despair of loneliness that comes with the awful specter of hatred; and we see in a small way the desperate reaching out for human love and acceptance. If we look very closely, we see how logic is twisted into "psycho-logic," that peculiar, distorted, and bizarre kind of reasoning that goes on in the dark hinterlands of the human soul. It is a kind of logic that is common to all of us, not just the harried and miserable neurotic. We see it in the clumsy defenses of our attitudes toward unwanted neighbors; toward members of racial and national groups that are not to our liking; in the way that we regard those of a different faith; and in the myriad of other defensive rationalizations that we employ to screen our true feelings from our conscious selves.

One of the most difficult and perplexing paradoxes encountered in working with unhappy and maladjusted people is the manner in which they seem to cling to obsessive, parasitic, and even pathological feelings despite what these feelings do to them. In ordinary conversation as well as in interview therapy they will admit with startling frankness that these anarchical feelings make them miserable, confused, anxious, and at times even angry. The anarchy of feeling by which they are constantly disturbed makes them feel inadequate, isolated, lonely, and alienated from the rest of their fellowmen. They recognize readily enough that such feelings cause much ego-damage, that they corrode self-respect, and that they undermine any real capacity for more positive feelings and the relations that spring from them. In brief, the anarchy of parasitic feeling results eventually in a total *emotional emasculation* which impoverishes the affective life of the person and destroys his ability to develop healthy interpersonal relationships with the people around him.

Thus in the drawing room no less than in the counseling center we repeatedly come up against the big question: Why do these unhuman, unwanted, and parasitic feelings persist over a span of countless years, sometimes even for a lifetime? Why do they cling like a leech to the mind of the harried person, sucking away the very marrow of his noblest thoughts and sentiments? Wouldn't you think that any person, facing the horror of his own hatred, guilt, or hostility, would spew these feelings out of his system as he would a deadly poison?

But the plain fact is that he doesn't. On the contrary, because of a strange, perverse psycho-logic, he actually seems to cling to them, just as they cling to him, even when he knows and is willing to recognize their parasitic and destructive qualities. Therefore, in order to understand what is going on in this strange subterranean arena of the human mind, we have to turn our question around. In place of the question, "What do obsessive and parasitic feelings do *to* people?" we should ask, "What do these feelings do *for* the person?" It is obvious that they must do something for him; otherwise he wouldn't cling to them so desperately, even when he is paying a substantial fee to a therapist to get rid of them. Let us see what these gains are.

Before analyzing some of the feelings that we have encountered in the previous pages of this story of human frailty and suffering, let us examine briefly the differences between logic and what we have called psycho-logic. All of us like to pride ourselves on the ability to think logically, to arrive at conclusions that are based on sound premises, and to follow the laws of logical deduction. Almost everyone is aware that logic is a *practical* discipline, a "normative science" which seeks to establish rules for clear-headed, correct thinking. It is a science that tests validity by objective facts, rational premises, and demonstrable hypotheses, by processes of rational deduction and inference, and especially by realistic thinking. Thus, if I can establish the fact that it is raining, it is logical to conclude that something somewhere is getting wet. It is logical and realistic to conclude, on the basis of current evidence, that the span of life will continue to increase, but not to some indefinite point which would guarantee immortality in this life.

This is the way that logic works; but not so in the murky realm of psycho-logic. This pale and distorted image of rational logic has little reference to fact, or reason, or testable premises. Instead, its peculiar format is based on the basic need of survival, and survival at any price. Its principles, if we may dignify them by such a term, are derived from the insatiable craving for ego-security, and for the ever-present demand within the personality to cope with reality no matter what the cost. It is this kind of subterranean illogic that not only underwrites the anarchy of feeling in all its ramifications but also spawns the growth of neurotic and psychotic symptoms. And, needless to say, it is this type of perverted logic which undermines or prevents the process of logical thinking.

Here is one of the most basic reasons why the anarchy of feeling manages to maintain a stranglehold on the personality and its reactions. It explains why the faculty of reason is so weak and ineffectual in the person dominated by feeling. Time and again in psychotherapy we hear the childish plaint: "I know that I shouldn't think this way, that it's wrong, that it's contrary to reason. But my feelings won't let me look at it any other way." I feel, I feel, I feel, is the unending monotonous refrain of the person who has sacrificed reason to the anarchy of feeling.

The unrealistic and bizarre logic common to persons whose feelings are uncontrolled is supported by a number of other characteristics that play an important part in maintaining the anarchy of feeling. Feelings, no matter how bad or destructive, are retained and even nurtured because *they are a part of the personality*. They have a time-honored quality about them in that they reach back into early childhood, and thus they are familiar, comfortable, and even safe. Moreover, powerful feelings like hatred help to polarize one's strivings —actually to give meaning and purpose to life—and in this strange way to forge some degree of ego strength and integration. Everyone can think of men like Hitler and Stalin whose whole purpose in life seemed to revolve around hatred. Without this hatred their lives would have had no meaning, and as long as this focal point remained they were able to function in a way that was never predicted of them.

We may note further that the peculiar logic of negative feelings is supported by the fact that they often function as substitutes for positive feelings. The logic here is that "any feelings are better than no feelings at all," a conclusion that happens to have some realistic support. Hostility, inferiority, anxiety, or hatred at least keep alive the conviction that life is still going on, and that in some cases it even has directionality. Inferiority may make life difficult, but apathy (or no feeling) makes it unbearable. Even negative feelings, derived as they are in the course of time from the more natural, positive feelings with which nature endows the human mind, have some life-giving properties to them. They are like nitroglycerin to the cardiac patient. The pounding headache that sometimes results from the ingestion of the drug is much more acceptable than death.

This fact, that negative feelings are ultimately derived from positive, healthy feelings, is important in re-establishing the primacy of reason. Hostility, after all, is a derivative of anger, just as anxiety is a derivative of fear. And when people begin to realize that anger has a definite place in the scheme of human response, they begin to see more clearly why hostility *does not*. Love is a wondrous emotion, set by nature to enrich the lives of those whom it favors in good proportion. But possessiveness and jealousy and lust have nothing in their favor. They tyrannize and eventually destroy the personality on which they feed parasitically for as long as they are tolerated.

There is one additional quality of the logic of feeling that we may note in order to complete our account of how psychologic works. Negative feelings are often used by the hapless victim to justify the misery of his existence. Having lost his orientation to real and worthwhile values, and having sacrificed the meaning of life on the altar of momentary experience, he turns to his feelings to explain why his personal life is so unhappy. This, he consoles himself, is why my life is so intolerable. If only I did not feel the way I do—so anxious, so inferior, so inadequate, so insecure, and so on—things would become better, and life would again have a real meaning. But then his perverse logic warns him that without these feelings his life would still be without purpose or meaning and therefore he must safeguard them at all costs. This is the form of psycho-logic. This is the anarchy of feeling in its starkest portrayal.

Let us now look a little more closely at the psycho-logic of some of the destructive feelings that we described in earlier chapters. Let us look first at the feeling dimension of hatred-hostility and see what it does for its victim in contrast to what it does to him.

The one thing that we can be immediately sure of is that hatred, and its paler companion hostility, serve very effectively to protect one's self from contact with, and especially obligations to, the hated person. We began this chapter with a quotation taken straight from the lexicography of psycho-logic: "I hate him, and I'm glad I hate him, because if I didn't hate him I might like him, and I hate him." As the client referred to earlier said of his hated uncle, "I hate him, all right, but I still wouldn't let him know it. I want him to like me, despite the fact that I hate him. Maybe I don't really hate him after all, but I don't like to think of this because it would take a lot of meaning out of my life. I don't know exactly how I would function without this feeling. I certainly wouldn't know how to react to that uncle of mine."

Similarly, hostility can be used quite effectively to ward off social relationships and the development of friendships. There is nothing more effective than hostility to keep people at a distance, the whole idea being that at a distance they cannot again inflict the pain that someone once did. If you have nothing to do *with* people, they can do nothing *to* you. The risk is much too great, and therefore hostility must be maintained and nurtured in order to avoid the terrible pain of rejection, scorn, ridicule, or possessive love. This reminds us of another attitude encountered so frequently in therapeutic counseling which might be called the "failure" attitude. In such instances the logic is again impeccable, even though it is basically unrealistic. "If I do not try," says the victim of the failure attitude, "I cannot fail. And I would do anything rather than fail. Inaction is bad enough, but failure is destructive and completely intolerable." As you can see, in each instance psycho-logic is used most effectively to achieve illogical or unrealistic aims.

There is of course the fact that hatred can be used, and often is used, for personal gratification. "He hurt me very badly," wails the victim of hatred, "and I can only get satisfaction by hating him. I would like to hurt him in the same way. I would even like to destroy him. But this I cannot do because of its consequences, and so I will accept the best substitute possible—hatred. I know that hatred is destructive, but the chances are that it will destroy him just as quickly as it destroys me."

Perhaps the most bizarre example of the kind of logic that we are examining is that in which hatred of another is used to obscure and project hatred of self. Self-rejection, self-alienation, and self-hatred are very painful and damaging to any personality. At times this feeling toward self becomes so intense and pervasive that it is intolerable; and in such instances it becomes psychologically imperative to hide this fact from one's self. The surest way to do this is to project the hatred onto another person or onto society in general. This is a form of personal scapegoating by which the pain and degradation of self-hatred are overcome by finding a scapegoat in whom the venom of hatred can be injected. It is only when such persons reject this self-alienation and rejoin the brotherhood of man through a positive act of self-love that hatred and hostility can be dissipated. The ramparts of hatred have to be stormed by the battalions of love, or hatred will eventually destroy all those who become its victims.

In each instance of the anarchy of negative feeling, the logic is much the same, although it may be twisted to suit the demands of a particular situation. When we examine the psycho-logic of insecurity and inferiority feelings, we find that its essential function is to defend and protect. The feeling of insecurity cries out for help, that is, it is expressly designed to achieve safety and to insure freedom from threat and anxiety. Thus it causes its victim to build all sorts of psychological emplacements that serve to ward off attacks against security. If it is financial security you're worried about, take out another endowment policy; if it's health, take more vitamins; if it's your job, invite the boss out to dinner and make much of him.

In this analysis of the purpose of insecurity, we see the logic of anxiety also. Anxiety is the conscious expression of the feeling of insecurity, and thus the two reflect the same kind of logic. Anxiety is of its nature protective. It is a danger sign that warns the individual that something had better be done about a threatening situation. And this is good—if the anxiety doesn't get out of hand. In the normal person anxiety works rather well and stays within bounds; but in the inadequate personality in whom there is a great deal of insecurity, anxiety not only gets out of hand but becomes "free-floating," which means that the person has become the victim of a feeling that has no rational logic to it. Normal anxiety is a derivative of normal fear; abnormal anxiety is *a derivative of insecurity*.

The feeling of insecurity is closely allied to inferiority, which is one of the most common, pervasive, and crippling feelings ever encountered. No one likes to feel inferior, as any victim will gladly tell you; yet there is a sweet taste to the pity, the support, and the succor that it often elicits from other people. It is also very useful as a device to excuse personal failure, although this psycho-logic occurs more often in connection with the feeling of inadequacy. Inferiority, on the other hand, is used to rationalize the performance that is poorer than that of others, and it also serves the purpose of enhancing a positive feeling that results when actual accomplishment occurs, as it does occasionally. The deeper the inferiority the stronger the taste of success.

Generally, however, inferiority interferes with successful accomplishment, and the deeper it is buried, the more it tends to generate paradoxical attitudes of superiority and perfectionism, and to utilize the mechanisms of projection and blaming. These developments support the inferiority because in the one case it makes the person feel more important and worthwhile (superiority or perfectionism), whereas in the other it enables him to get rid of the blame that is associated with inadequate performance or failure. We need hardly add that the logic of insecurity, inferiority, and inadequacy unites the three feelings in a triumvirate of anarchy which often cripples the personality beyond effective repair.

In a similar vein, the distortions of love already referred to as possessiveness and jealousy, and the caricatures of self-love which masquerade as envy and pride, can be analyzed in a way to reveal their support in the logic of the unconscious. The specter of possessiveness, especially as it is manifested in "smother" love, is obviously supported by the legal premise that "possession is nine points of the law," and therefore no one can take "it" away from me. Jealousy works in much the same way, although it has its roots more in anger and fear than does possessiveness. The feeling of jealousy acts to prevent any intrusion into the domain of a personal relationship, and thus sets a rigid limit on the behavior of other persons ensnared by it. The jealous husband makes sure that his attractive wife sees no one but him by eliminating everyone else from the scene with his rages and tantrums. Jealousy is closely allied to the feeling of mistrust which serves its own purpose of eliminating any risk where the behavior of other people is concerned. By thoroughly mistrusting other people, one can be sure never to become the victim of human frailty. By the same rule, of course, mistrust also excludes the noblest of human sentiments, such as acceptance, liking, trust, and friendship.

In this category can also be included the strangling emotions of envy and greed. There is perhaps no person more miserable than one who cannot tolerate the good fortunes of others. His envy is at times all-consuming, and for this reason it is often confused with jealousy. Both of these feelings are so powerful that they pervade every part of one's psychic life, and thus produce the "blindness" that is often associated with strong emotions. They are obviously excellent examples of the anarchy of feeling. But jealousy is always directed toward something already possessed, whereas envy is just the opposite and is stimulated by something not possessed. It is, however, this relationship to possession that makes them so similar and explains why they are often confused with one another.

Both of them are also much alike in their disruptive effects on other feelings, on logical and realistic thinking, and on interpersonal relationships. But there is some divergence in the logic that it used to support them. The jealous person, as we have seen, uses his jealousy unconsciously to protect himself from intrusion or loss; the envious person utilizes his envy to mask his own hostility. You can see that in envy there is much anger, and it is this anger that the envious person wishes to deny. Envy is of course the contrary of love, since love creates generosity and good will, which are conspicuously absent in the envious person.

There is little difference between envy and greed, since it is clear that the greedy person, like his envious counterpart, wants what someone else has. The psycho-logic of greed is quite apparent, its principal aim being personal gain. It, too, is related to possession and thus, along with jealousy and envy, functions as a malevolent triumvirate within the anarchy of feeling. It is manifestly destructive of psychological health, positive feelings, and healthy relationships with other people. As always with such destructive feelings, it acts quickly to topple reason from its throne.

Finally, we may take as a focal point for study the destructive feelings of guilt and shame. Here again we encounter a pair of concepts like jealousy and envy, inferiority and inadequacy, that are in some respects so similar that most people find it hard to tell them apart. The fact that the same act, generally an immoral or anti-social one, will arouse both feelings at the same time lends a great deal of weight to this similarity. The reason for this is that both of these feelings involve the ego in much the same way, causing it to feel degraded, worthless, and of little value in the opinions of others.

But it is just here that we are able to make a useful distinction between guilt and shame. Of the two, shame is the more ego-centered and therefore potentially the more destructive. It is extremely painful and may become intolerable because it involves not only deep self-rejection but, even more importantly, the *anticipated rejection of others*. It is difficult at times to face ourselves in the mirror of reflection and self-analysis; but it is *impossible*, at least for most people, to tolerate the scourge of social disapproval, rejection, or ostracism. This is why exposure is regarded with such intense dread by persons (like homosexuals) whose behavior or "sins" are so far out of line with social mores. This is also the reason why the mechanism of rationalization is practically universal. Rationalization—that is, finding excuses for our bad behavior—helps greatly to reduce the psychic pain that is always associated in such large quantities with the feeling of shame.

Guilt, on the other hand, is not as strongly ego-oriented as shame, although it is potentially very destructive of psychological health. But guilt—as least in its normal form—is partly oriented toward the wrongful act and partly toward our objective obligations to others. It is for this reason that ordinary guilt—the feeling that we experience when we deliberately violate some rule of conduct or social norm—amounts to little more than a personal conviction of wrongdoing and an internal demand for setting things straight again. Once this is done, the feeling of guilt generally disappears without leaving any scratches, blemishes, or scars on the somewhat delicate epidermis of the ego. Guilt in this sense of the term is nothing more than a reflection of the fact that our conscience can distinguish right from wrong, and that most people are willing to accept the idea that whatever is wrong morally or socially should be avoided.

The kind of guilt to which we referred earlier is a much more serious problem, and has all of the damaging and parasitic qualities that other negative feelings have. It is derived not from the conviction of wrongdoing but rather from the conviction of *personal evil, wickedness, or worthlessness.* This kind of guilt is abnormal and pathological and clearly belongs within the framework of the anarchy of feeling. In its effect on the integrity of the ego it closely resembles its partner, shame.

Why, then, should we harbor such feelings? What is the logic behind guilt and shame? Well, for one thing, as Freud pointed out, abnormal guilt is actually a reflection of the *need for punishment,* and the *need to feel punished,* both of which are assured by the sense of guilt. The primary aim of neurotic guilt is to secure punishment, and the psycho-logic behind this is the fact that punishment is necessary to expiate the guilt, to drive it out of the mind so as to ward off ego-destruction. "I am evil and degraded and worthless," cries the unhappy victim, "and therefore I feel guilty and I should be punished. I am no good to anyone and I should be rejected. Even God cannot love someone as worthless as I am."

In this tragic statement—one that every therapist will recognize from his own experience—we see how the unconscious logic of guilt works on its victim. He is worthless and therefore he *should* be rejected, and his guilt assures him of this rejection. At the same time, his deep feeling of shame will assure his own *self-rejection,* and thus the unhappy victim, rejected by society and imprisoned by his own feelings, experiences the loneliness of the complete outcast. He is alone in the world, alienated from self and, as he sees it, alienated from society because of his particular anarchy of feeling. He dare not rid himself of the guilt, no matter how destructive it becomes, because it is the only way in which he can rationalize his worthlessness, and it offers the only hope for redemption through punishment. The psycho-logic of guilt and shame is one of the most dramatic instances of the distortion of thinking that can occur in the interest of maintaining the anarchy of feeling. This is psycho-logic in its most destructive form.

From this brief excursion into the deeper recesses of the unconscious mind and its peculiar, twisted logic, we can learn an important lesson—one that we hope to spell out more completely in our final chapter. This lesson centers on the important fact that all people—normal or neurotic, well-balanced or off-balance—want to be reasonable and to act rationally even when they are not always succeeding in doing so. They yearn for logical principles of living even to the extent that at times they have to make up some of their own. There is a deep unshakable conviction in the human mind that it is better to act logically than to act illogically; that it is better to be rational than irrational; that it is better to be sound than unsound. This is both the rationale and the justification of rational counseling and psychotherapy. Certainly, if the human mind cannot transcend feeling and re-establish rationality, there is little hope for either counseling or psychotherapy.

11 | REASON VERSUS ANARCHY

I was angry with my foe:
I told it not, my wrath did grow.

—BLAKE.

IN THIS SOMEWHAT circuitous voyage through the labyrinth of human feelings, and through our exploration of the caves in which we found the dry bones of psycho-logic, we have finally come full circle. We are back to a question which has plagued us from the start of our journey, and that is, In what way can reason regain dominion over the anarchy of feeling? How can reason be pitted successfully against the strangulation of mind and behavior caused by emotion? How can the revolt against reason be turned back and instinctual man put in his proper place?

Let us retrace our steps for just a brief while and see what we have learned in our study of this psychic anarchy. We began with a basic premise which was exemplified again and again in each succeeding chapter: feeling uncontrolled leads to anarchy in human behavior and in human relationships. The concept of anarchy was used to signify analogously what is meant by it in political science. It is a state of confusion without government or law; it is disorder due to absence of control or restraint. This is how the dictionary defines anarchy from a political viewpoint, and the concept can be just as easily applied to the realm of the mind.

It was hypothesized that feeling, when uncontrolled, leads to anarchy, to the dethronement of reason, and to loss of rational control over one's thinking, behavior, and personal relationships. This anarchy eventually generates crippling psychological mechanisms which are used to obscure, deny, and reduce the damage caused by feelings of guilt, inferiority, insecurity, and anxiety. In some instances, in the place of mechanisms, there is symptom-formation which serves much the same purpose. As we saw, symptoms are psychological devices which are developed for the sake of coping with the demands of reality, with everyday problems and conflicts, and with disturbing frustrations. This symptom-formation is but one step removed from well-known neurotic and psychotic developments which bring in their wake extreme confusion, disintegration of the personality, and disorientation to reality. These mechanisms and symptom-formations, along with neurotic and psychotic patterns, are the expression of psychological thinking—the kind of pathological and distorted thinking that is formulated in the unconscious, is dictated by needs and traumatic experiences, and serves the demands of feeling rather than objective evidence or reason.

The evidence for this interpretation of the anarchy of feeling and psycho-logical thinking was derived in large measure from clinical case histories, but is securely supported by personal experience, mounting psychological disorders, marital maladjustment, increase in juvenile delinquency and crime, and other phenomena that are expressions of the dethronement of human reason. The anarchy of feeling is of course the other side of the coin, so that when reason is abandoned and feeling is allowed to run amok, anarchy is the only outcome that can be expected.

We must do whatever we can to reverse this trend, because

of the millions of persons who are adversely affected by the failure to live an intelligent and reasonable existence, and by the damaging effect that this failure has on human society. The millions of unhappy and disturbed persons, including neurotics and psychotics, alcoholics and drug addicts, criminals and psychopaths, unhappily married and lonely unmarried persons, cry out for help. "Tell us," they plead, "how we can untangle ourselves from the skein of human emotion. What can we do to regain control of our feelings? How can we utilize the God-given instrument of reason in order to live a reasonable life?" These are the tragic questions encountered every day by the minister and priest, by the psychologist and psychiatrist, by parent and friend. They are the most challenging questions that any of us face at the present time, and we must do whatever we can to provide answers for them.

Let it be understood, as we have emphasized time and time again, that feelings and emotions have a definite role in the human scheme of things. Feelings are needed to enrich our lives and to add depth to the meaning of existence. Emotions like anger, fear, and anxiety are necessary to security, safety, and getting things done. The emotion of love is as necessary to the health of the mind as food is to the body. Feelings like admiration, respect, reverence, sorrow, and remorse transform the pale façade of ordinary existence into a vibrant and living thing. Without pride and passion, sympathy and sorrow, the dull moments of time would tick off an endless eternity of worldly existence. In every phase of human existence, in every moment of time, we find countless instances of the enrichment of life by feeling and emotions.

Similarly, we see countless instances of the tragic impact of the absence of feeling. The dull, unresponsive, apathetic person is unable to respond to the world in which he lives. The cadences of music or the rhythms of poetry have no particular meaning for him, and the laughter of children or the joy of Christmas leaves him unmoved. Small wonder that schizophrenia, the most crippling of mental diseases, is characterized by emotional apathy. On the other side of the picture is the psychopath who also is apathetic, but in his own way. In him there is no vestige of sympathy, or remorse, or love, or guilt. There is just an emptiness, a void. Where feeling might have taken root and developed, there is nothing that enables the miserable victim to respond in a human way to the joys and tragedies, the hopes and the despairs of human existence. It is hard to tell who is in the poorer position, the neurotic crippled and bowed down by his anarchy of feeling, or the psychopath who does not know what human feeling is like. But of one thing we can be sure, and that is that both of these unhappy people are somewhat less than human, because their feelings and emotions have not been integrated into the stream of human response.

This anarchy of feeling, whether instigated by a pathological apathy or by a parasitic strangulation, is opposed unequivocally to the primacy of reason. Where feeling dominates the thinking, behavior, or relationships of men, reason cannot function effectively. This means essentially that there must be a proper place for both feeling and reason in the lives and conduct of human beings. Where there are no feelings humanity is impoverished and distorted; where there is an excess of feeling the quality of being human is attenuated and impoverished. There is need, then, to integrate feeling into the totality of human existence; there is a need for domination and control in order for feeling to assume its proper and rightful place in the pattern of human relationships.

It is clear that we are dealing here with an essential problem in psychology and philosophy—*the nature of man.* If man is primarily and essentially a feeling creature, and only secondarily rational, then life should be properly dominated by feeling and only conditioned to a degree by reason. But if man is primarily a rational being, with feeling existing only as a complement to his rational nature, then reason should hold the position of primacy and should, in all situations, exercise dominion and control over feelings and emotions. As one unhappy girl expressed it very succinctly: "I know what I should do. I know that what I am doing is immoral and indecent. I know that I am acting contrary to all of the laws and principles of society and religion. All of this my reason tells me, and all of this I have heard time and time again from my parents, teachers, and friends. But I don't want to do what is good and right. I find this kind of life extremely boring. When I act the way I feel like acting, I am myself, and not some caricature created by the demands of my parents, the rules of society, or the Commandments of God. Only when I act the way I feel like acting do I feel that I am really existing. And I don't really care whether I become psychotic, derelict, or damned."

Here, again, we see the anarchy of feeling in sharp outline. Here we see the eternal human conflict between reason and passion, between the "ought" of morality and the lusts of the flesh. In this naked statement of an eighteen-year-old girl— whose I.Q. was 146—we encounter the anarchy of feeling and the dethronement of reason in its starkest form. And it is this kind of situation that forces us to take a position regarding the nature of man. If this young psychopath is right, then reason must take a back seat in the affairs of men. Unfortunately, when reason is relegated to a lesser place, human life and human relationships begin to rot and to decay. Whether or not we like the restrictions of law or of reason, to be truly human and maintain our shaky link with the angels, we *have* to accept and learn to live by the rule of reason. Without this acceptance and this willingness we descend quickly into the dark cavern of license, libertinism, and mental disorder.

The big question, of course, is how the primacy of reason is established. For a complete answer we must go back to the period of childhood, because it is in the training of children that the groundwork is laid for a sane and reasonable existence. In the training of children, there stands out sharply a primary requirement of later mental health, and this is discipline. Not the kind of "discipline" that occurs as a distorted caricature of the real thing—including harsh and unjust punishment, repeated deprivation, withholding of love, or sadistic criticism—but discipline that is directed *toward order* in the child's life. For this is what discipline really means—*the establishment of order*. And order, we may note, is the direct antithesis of anarchy. Healthy, constructive discipline in childhood will inevitably pave the way for mental health in adulthood, and for that inner control of impulses and feeling that is so important to personal integration and a creative life. As Bruce Catton has pointed out:

We don't emphasize self-denial very much these days, either for our children or for ourselves. Instead we concentrate on our wants. We seem to have the notion that the world owes us all manner of good things, and we feel abused when we don't get them. Self-discipline is a bore; and as a result we are perilously close to winning an unwelcome fame as a land known for its spoiled children and discontented adults.*

Contrariwise, and in defiance of the law of discipline, we

* *Words To Live By*, ed. by William L. Nichols (New York, Simon and Schuster, 1959), p. 117. Copyright by Simon and Schuster, Inc.

often see in childhood the anarchy of feeling in its primitive form. A striking example is the explosion of behavior into temper tantrums, where feeling runs unbridled until exhaustion puts an end to things. We see anarchy also in the hostility and acting-out behavior of deeply angry children whose slowly growing psyche, struggling for existence and a secure hold on reality, is all but shattered by lack of love, parental desertion, or family breakdown. You see these tragic little victims lashing out with destructive behavior (biting, kicking, clawing, or destroying) that has all the earmarks of feeling run wild.

You see the same anarchy in the terror-filled eyes of the child who has been left alone for a long period of time, or the one who wakes up screaming with fear because of the stark terror of his dream. You see it in the incessant efforts of some children to gain attention or to secure love at any cost. You see it also in the schizoid child who is frightened by the prospect of leaving home, or being torn away from the security of the mother. These are but a few instances of the anarchy of feeling in childhood, but they are common ones and clearly exemplify the importance of bringing order and discipline and control into the lives of children if the primacy of reason is to have a secure beginning.

Mental health and personal integration, which stand opposed to emotional anarchy, can be given a strong forward push during adolescence by helping young men and women achieve maturity. Maturity is of course the cornerstone of adulthood, and of its very nature leaves little room for lack of behavior control or emotional disruption. To develop this important quality, the adolescent must also succumb to the demands of discipline, and many studies of adolescents indicate that this is just exactly what they want. The adolescent is keenly aware of the dangerous implications of loss of control. His own impulses and passions frighten him; his conflicts with parents and other authority figures are very disturbing; and he knows with a sureness that is sometimes startling that the only real antidote to these disabling influences is a disciplined existence.

As in childhood, the anarchy of feeling is sharply defined in the behavior of many teenagers. As almost any youngster will tell you, sexual feelings and impulses often get out of hand, the amount of guilt is sometimes unbearable, scrupulosity is unrelenting in its torment, and there is often a great deal of anxiety and confusion with respect to present events and future possibilities. For many other adolescents there are strange and disturbing homosexual tendencies that seem at times to be beyond control and that erupt into the most damaging kinds of behavior and personal relationships. In still others there is unbridled hostility and hatred which they cannot understand and find impossible to control, and which lead to all sorts of rebellion against parents, society, and God. In these unhappy and disturbed adolescents we see the anarchy of feeling in its most vicious form, twisting and distorting judgment and reason until the hapless youngster is brought to the brink of depression, despair, or self-destruction. Working with these youngsters, one cannot easily escape the conclusion that the primacy of reason and an orderly existence are the prime requisites of a healthy, productive life.

The need for rational control is obviously just as prominent in adult life as in childhood and adolescence. The demands of marriage, of one's job, of social relationships, of one's vocation, or of religious practices are such that without reason and discipline they are all likely to fall apart. Certainly, it must be obvious to everyone that countless marriages are destroyed by hostility, jealousy, or rage. Other social relationships break apart just as quickly under the impact of feelings of envy, hostility, or inferiority. And many a good job has gone sour because of hatred for one's boss or feelings of persecution.

The anarchy of feeling in adulthood is reflected in many facets of behavior. The impatient mother, the spinster who fears the onrush of age, the wife who is terrified by the implications of menopause, the oldster who is chronically anxious about his job, the young man who is driven into frenzy by uncontrolled ambition, the fifty-year-old man who fears loss of sexual power, or the suburbanite who is driven frantic by the need for status—all reflect a lack of reasonable control. These persons are victims of the anarchy of feeling, and will in time break out with characteristic mechanisms, symptoms, and disturbed behavior patterns. They, too, know that reason is the only antidote to this kind of personality rot, but too often feeling has successfully dethroned reason and keeps it securely bound by promising its victim more delightful things. That is why pleasure—an important and worthwhile value in itself—always serves as a handmaid to human feelings.

To offset these powerful influences, and thus contain feeling and pleasure within the bounds of reasonable control, it is necessary throughout all stages of development to nourish the growth of those elements of personality that help maintain the primacy of reason. Many things come to mind in this connection. All persons engaged in the practice of counseling and psychotherapy recognize that mental health and personal integration require a basically sound scale of values. Values are the very stuff of human reasoning, and without a healthy value system it is all but impossible for a person to cope with the demands and hardships, the tragedies and frustrations of daily life. To know what is good and worthwhile, and to strive actively for it, is as important to healthy living as good food, fresh air, or exercise. One must also develop and nourish healthy attitudes—toward self, toward others, toward reality, toward God, toward life. Egoism must make room for other-centeredness, and self-rejection, with its handmaids of shame, guilt, and self-hatred, must give way to self-acceptance. There is no room in the healthy mind for cynicism, pessimism, and all the other "isms" that poison human thought and generate crippling feelings.

There must also be continuous development of spiritual resources and of those virtues on which mental health so deeply depends. No one has ever discovered any acceptable alternatives for courage, patience, compassion, fortitude, charity, or temperance. These are some of the truly great virtues about which the ancients wrote most eloquently and which modern man too often forgets, or worse still, fails to become acquainted with. The dominion of reason also requires practical ideals, sound principles, and realizable goals to bulwark the mind against the ravages of feeling. This is the kind of nourishment that the human soul needs for the achievement and maintenance of a reasonable existence. These are the things without which mental health and personal integration are almost impossible. They stand securely in the way of the anarchy of feeling.

There are times of course, too many of them, when it becomes necessary to attempt to *re-establish* the primacy of reason because feeling has gained the upper hand and control has largely disappeared. There are countless people—the maladjusted, the unhappy, the rebellious, the neurotic, the delinquent—who for some reason have failed to achieve control and discipline, and who have become the unwilling victims of their own impulses and feelings. For them there is only one road open—the dissolution of anarchy and the reestablishment of reason. This is a hard thing to do, and unfortunately many persons who have appealed for help have found that their feelings are too deeply embedded, or the skill of the therapist too inadequate, to alter successfully the situation. This is a fact that we must face, but we cannot afford to let it stop us from applying whatever art or skill we do possess for the lessening of human misery.

In the unremitting search of the psychological scientist for techniques and skills with which to do battle against the spectre of mental disorder, various approaches have been used with varying success, ranging all the way from ordinary education and guidance to tranquilizers and shock therapy. The simplest of these approaches are the time-honored processes of education and guidance (including advice-giving), which have certainly mitigated the spread of maladjustment. As Gilbert Highet says, "But another aim of education, equally important or more important, is to train the individual mind as intensely and to encourage it as variously as possible—since much of our better and our more essential life is lived by us as individuals, and since (in the advancing age of mass-culture) it is vital for us to maintain personal independence."* In point of fact, following up this thought, if education (and its counterpart, guidance) were to do a near-perfect job—the kind of job that all educators wish for and know that they cannot possibly accomplish—there would be much less unhappiness, disorder, or maladjustment in this world of ours. The very aim of education is to so form the mind and personality of students that problems and difficulties, conflicts and frustra-

* Gilbert Highet, *Man's Unconquerable Mind* (New York, Columbia University Press, 1954), p. 76.

tions, can be handled, if not with consummate ease, at least with a great deal of skill.

Unhappily, this sort of thing rarely happens, either because of limitations within human personality, or weaknesses in the educational process; and so we must turn to other things whenever ordinary processes of growth and development have failed, and neurosis or something worse has gained control of the personality. It is then that we turn to counseling, psychotherapy, or medical treatment.

In a book of this scope we cannot go far into the intricacies of counseling and psychotherapy, about which huge volumes and hundreds of articles have been written. Nor will we attempt to distinguish too precisely these two intricate processes for the reader. Let us be content with the simple statement that psychological counseling is aimed essentially at an increase of human freedom for the individual client, and thus is particularly well suited to a reduction of the anarchy of feeling. Counseling can be effectively used to help the client get rid of certain blocks, frustrations, and sensitivities in his personality, and to lift the yoke of parasitic feelings so that the person is in a better position to move toward acceptable goals and to play an active part in shaping his own destiny.

Psychotherapy has much the same aims, but reaches, as it were, deeper into the hidden recesses of personality in order to come to grips with those psychic hindrances that prevent the patient from using his distinctively human capacities. It delves into the unconscious and into the past; it analyzes dreams and symptoms; it explores and probes into early relationships in order to find out why this personality is what it is, and how it might be freed of traumatic experiences, crippling mechanisms, pathological feelings, or a rigid symptomatology. Psychotherapy strives to understand the logic of symptoms and the psycho-logic of unconscious thinking. It tries to relate the formation of the child to the behavior of the adult. In all of this it is dominated by one primary aim: the restoration of mental health and the re-establishment of rational control.

All of this might sound very complicated, and sometimes it is; but in both counseling and psychotherapy it is necessary to help the client or the patient to become aware of his own feelings and what these feelings mean to him. There must be an opportunity for the expression of feeling, for what the therapist calls abreaction and acting-out, so that the patient will have a chance to "get it out of his system." The person must learn to relinquish the benefits of feeling, in exactly the same way that the normal person must in many instances learn to forego pleasure for the sake of higher goals. The hatred of one's parents may taste sweet, but so do a lot of poisonous substances that will kill if taken internally.

Counseling and psychotherapy must also help to undermine the psycho-logic of feeling and help the client to understand why he clings to destructive feelings even when he knows them to be destructive. Becoming aware of their peculiar and bizarre logic, the person is then in a position to break their strangle hold on his personality.

It is through such techniques as these, and others, that the anarchy of feeling can be finally destroyed. Gradually the client regains control of feeling, and with this control comes the re-establishment of reason and sanity. Only in this way can man live the distinctively human life for which he was equipped by Nature. In his never-ending effort to move toward higher goals of production and creativity man must learn how to use reason against anarchy, regardless of whether this anarchy is political or psychological.

GLOSSARY

ABERRATION—Deviation from that which is usual or normal.

ABNORMAL—Different from the usual, average, or normal; sometimes used to mean pathological.

ABREACTION—Release or discharge of painful emotions leading to desensitization and increased insight.

ADJUSTMENT—The psychological process of coping with internal and external demands, conflicts, frustrations, stresses, and problems by means of some personal response.

AFFECTIVE—Pertaining to feelings and emotions.

AGGRESSION (AGGRESSIVENESS)—Hostile tendency or action; behavior that brings the aggressor into forceful contact with another organism or object; also, any psychological equivalent for such an attack.

AMBIVALENCE—Contradictory feelings or attitudes toward persons, things, or relationships, experienced simultaneously.

ANACHRONISM—An event occurring out of its proper time, as the use of horses in an age of tractors.

ANXIETY—Fearfulness or apprehension regarding oneself or some external event. It is often intense and disturbing. When no real danger or threat exists it is called neurotic anxiety.

APATHY—Emotional indifference, or a marked absence of feeling or emotion in situations that ordinarily call for such responses.

CARDIAC—Pertaining to the heart.

COMPENSATION—A defensive mechanism which is used to obscure or to counter-balance personal defects and inadequacies.

COMPULSION—A strong and sometimes irresistible impulse to perform some act or ritual even though it is conceived to be unreasonable, as in compulsive hand-washing.

CONFLICT—A state of mind, sometimes prolonged, that results from a clash between contrary motivations. It may be conscious or unconscious, internal or external.

CONSCIENCE—The capacity of the human mind to distinguish right from wrong; it is the intellect directed toward the morality of human acts.

CONTINUUM—A continuous, unbroken series, or whole.

CROSS-IDENTIFICATION—Identification with a member of the opposite sex, as in the case of a girl with her father.

DEFENSE MECHANISMS—Adjustive reactions, usually unconscious, designed to protect the person from his own limitations or from external stresses and frustrations.

DEPRESSION—A mental condition involving unpleasant feelings, emotional dejection, and a sense of foreboding.

DETERMINISM—A theory of human conduct according to which all conduct is regarded as a necessary outcome of antecedent causes and conditions.

DISINTEGRATION—The breaking down of a whole, such as personality, into its parts or functions; disunity or disharmony.

DISORIENTATION—A state of confusion about place, time, or personal identity.

DON JUAN—A type of seducer of women who enjoys more the feeling of conquest than the act of seduction itself. The term is used psychiatrically to denote compulsive sexual overactivity in males.

DYNAMICS—Pertaining to energy or force. In psychology, pertaining to those factors that influence or determine human behavior.

EGO—The whole person, the "I" of human experience. That part of the person that is directly involved in conscious experiences.

EGOCENTRISM—A psychological mechanism used to force recognition and to obscure personal inadequacy by boastfulness and self-aggrandizement.

EGO-INTEGRITY—A quality of the ego that insures internal harmony and consistency of response.

EGO-SECURITY—A personal quality that insures defense against stress, conflict, or frustration.

EGOTISM—(see egocentrism).

EMOTIONAL EMASCULATION—Impoverishment of feelings and emotions by excessive demands of another person or situation.

EMOTIONAL SECURITY—(see security, feeling of).

ETHNIC—Pertaining to a specific group or race.

EXISTENTIALISM—A doctrine midway between traditional materialism and idealism which stresses personal decision in a universe without purpose.

FRUSTRATION—The blocking of impulses, needs, drives, or behavior; also, hindrance in effecting adequate adjustment.

GUILT, SENSE OF—The feeling or conviction of having acted contrary to some principle, rule, or law. When unconscious and morbid, it is referred to as pathological or neurotic guilt.

HAND-WASHING COMPULSION—(see compulsion).

HEDONISM—The theory that pleasure is the primary aim or goal of all human conduct and striving.

HOMOSEXUALITY—Sexual attraction or relationship between members of the same sex.

HOSTILITY—A feeling or attitude, often unconscious, leading to behavior that is detrimental to individuals or groups against whom the hostility is directed.

HYPOCHONDRIA—Morbid concern about one's physical or mental health.

IDENTIFICATION—The unconscious assumption of similarity or identity with another person or a group for defensive purposes or the enhancement of prestige and personal worth.

ILLUSION—A false perception of reality.

IMPOTENCE—Inability to perform the sexual act usually due to failure of erection. Impotence is generally psychic in origin.

INFERIORITY, ATTITUDE OF—An attitude toward self, often unconscious, caused by inadequacy, lack of self confidence, or failure, and leading to unfavorable comparison with other persons.

INSENSATE—Without sense, feeling, or judgment.

INTEGRATION—A process or condition whereby diverse elements in any structure or system (like personality) are organized into a coordinated unity. Integration is basic to mental health and adjustment.

INVOLUTIONAL MELANCHOLIA—A psychotic reaction occurring during the involutional period of both men and women, characterized commonly by depression and sometimes by paranoid thinking. There may be feelings of guilt, anxiety, and delusional ideas.

JANSENISM—The doctrinal system of Cornelis Jansen, a Roman Catholic Bishop, which maintained the radical corruption of human nature and the inability of the will to do good. This doctrine is reflected in the attitude of many persons toward sex.

LIBERTINE—A person who acts without restraint or control, especially moral restraints; a licentious person.

MALADJUSTMENT—Inability to meet personal or environmental demands, and to resolve conflicts, frustrations, and problems in a wholesome or effective manner.

MASCULINE PROTEST—According to Adlerian theory, the desire to achieve masculine superiority as a cover-up for inferiority.

MATERIALISM—The philosophical viewpoint that matter is the only reality that exists; it contains the implicit denial of mind and spirit.

MATURITY—A terminal state of growth and development that promotes the healthy adjustment of the organism.

MECHANISM—In psychology, an acquired response by which ego qualities are maintained or protected without the use of choice or deliberation.

MENTAL HEALTH—A positive quality or state of mind (psyche) which enables a person to cope effectively with problems, conflicts, frustrations, and reality demands.

NEED—A tension aroused in the personality by the absence or deprivation of some object, quality, experience, or relationship required for personal well-being.

NEGATIVE IDENTIFICATION—The unconscious rejection of traits, attitudes, and qualities of another person or group with whom one is ordinarily closely related.

NEUROSIS—A relatively mild psychological disorder, the cause of which is psychic rather than physical. It is often referred to as psychoneurosis.

NEUROTIC—Pertaining to neurosis; a person suffering from a neurosis.

NEUROTIC ANXIETY—(see anxiety).

NEUROTIC GUILT—(see guilt).

NORMAL (NORMALITY)—Conforming to, or not deviating from, some acceptable norm, standard, or criterion. This norm may be statistical, moral, or psychological.

NYMPHOMANIA—Excessive and sometimes insatiable sex desire in women; corresponds to satyriasis in men.

OBSESSION—An idea or idea-complex with a strong emotional quality (usually unpleasant) that forces itself into and disturbs normal thought processes.

OEDIPUS COMPLEX—A psychoanalytic term used to designate an excessive love relationship between mother and son, which is accompanied by hostility toward the father.

ONTOLOGY (ONTOLOGICAL)—The philosophical discipline which studies the nature of being in all of its forms.

ORIENTATION—A particular outlook or viewpoint; also, good adjustment regarding time, place, and persons.

OVER-COMPENSATION—An excessive effort to overcome or reduce the damaging effects of inadequacy or inferiority.

PANACEA—A remedy for all diseases; a cure-all.

PARANOIA—A psychosis characterized by systematized fixed delusions (false beliefs), usually of a grandiose or persecutory nature.

PARASITIC—Pertaining to an animal or plant which lives on or in an organism of another species from which it obtains its nutriment. Thus, anything which clings to or feeds off something else.

PATHOLOGY—A branch of medicine which treats of the essential nature of disease, particularly as it is reflected in structural or functional changes in the organism.

Perfectionism—The neurotic trait or compulsion to be perfect, or to do everything perfectly; generally associated with feelings of inadequacy and inferiority.

Personality—The organized, emergent totality of characteristics, dispositions, mannerisms, and values that determine a person's adjustment to self and environment.

Phobia—A strong, morbid, persistent fear, usually of unknown origin.

Pragmatism—The philosophical viewpoint that the value or worth of anything is determined by its usefulness.

Projection—A psychological mechanism by which personal weaknesses, failures, and undesirable traits are attributed to external sources.

Promiscuity, Sexual—Sexual relationships with numerous and frequently changed partners. Also, sexual gratification without the element of love.

Psyche—The mind (or soul) as distinct from the body.

Psychiatry—A branch of medicine which is concerned with the diagnosis, treatment, and care of persons suffering from mental or personality disturbances.

Psychoanalysis—A theory and a method of treatment, originated by Sigmund Freud, relating to neurotic and other mental disorders.

Psycho-logic—Thinking or reasoning that is determined unconsciously by overpowering feelings.

Psychological Determinism—The theory that all human conduct results from such factors as feelings, needs, and habits, rather than from personal choices.

PSYCHOLOGICAL FREEDOM—Free will; free choice; the ability of the human person, when conditions are appropriate, to regulate or control his own responses.

PSYCHOLOGICAL HEALTH—(see mental health).

PSYCHOLOGICAL MECHANISM—(see mechanism).

PSYCHOLOGICAL NORMALITY—Behavior or personality makeup that conforms to standards of good adjustment, mental health, and efficiency.

PSYCHOPATHIC (PERSONALITY)—A term used to indicate a personality disorder characterized by weak character structure, impulsiveness, and emotional inadequacy.

PSYCHOSEXUAL—Pertaining to experiences or processes that are determined or conditioned by sexual needs and impulses.

PSYCHOSIS (PSYCHOTIC)—A severe emotional or personality disorder in which there is impairment of thinking, emotion, and behavior. Often characterized by loss of contact with reality and personality deterioration.

PSYCHOSOCIAL—Pertaining to processes or behavior that are determined partly by psychological and partly by social factors.

PSYCHOSOMATIC—Pertaining to mind and body taken as a unit; a specialized field of medical study that emphasizes the fundamental unity of mind and body. Also, pertaining to physical disorders caused by psychic factors.

PSYCHOTHERAPY—Any clinical process involving psychological methods, such as psychoanalysis or hypnosis, used to treat mental disorders by the reduction of symptoms and underlying causes.

PUNITIVE—Pertaining to any attitude or behavior that involves inflicting punishment.

RATIONALIZATION—A psychological mechanism by which a person justifies doubtful attitudes, beliefs, or actions by inventing spurious reasons and thus safeguarding his own ego.

REPRESSION—A psychological mechanism by which emotionally toned experiences, feelings, etc., are forced out of or prevented from coming into consciousness because of their undesirable or disturbing quality.

ROLE DIFFUSION—The dissipation or loss of personal identity by assuming too many different roles.

SADISM (SADISTIC)—Sexual abnormality in which sexual gratification is derived from the infliction of punishment or cruelty on another person.

SATYRIASIS—Abnormal and insatiable sexual desire in men, corresponding to nymphomania in women.

SCAPEGOATING—Projecting personal or social blame to others and causing them to suffer in place of the guilty person.

SCHIZOID—Pertaining to traits of shyness, introversion, and withdrawal which resemble schizophrenic characteristics.

SCHIZOPHRENIA—A severe, functional psychosis, characterized by loss of contact with reality, disorganized thinking, and emotional apathy.

SCRUPULOSITY—In its clinical form, a neurosis that is characterized by obsessive guilt and compulsive ritual; it is closely related to obsessive-compulsive neurosis.

SECURITY, FEELING OF—The deep conviction that one is able to cope with the problems and demands of reality.

SELF-CONCEPT—An individual's personal idea of himself, including his attitudes, values, ideals, and principles.

SELF-IDENTITY—A characteristic of the mature person who knows who he is, what he is, and the direction of his striving.

SEX-IDENTITY—The feeling or conviction of masculinity in the male and femininity in the female.

SHOCK THERAPY—A form of medical treatment of mental disorder which utilizes the shock effects produced by electrical impulses or the injection of insulin for the alleviation of distressing symptoms and for eventual cure.

SUPEREGO—In psychoanalysis, that part of the psychic structure that resembles the conscience. It is based upon the introjection of parental restrictions, demands, etc.

SYMBIOTIC—Pertaining to a condition or relationship which joins two organisms in such a way that one cannot live or function without the other.

SYMPTOMATOLOGY—The aggregate of symptoms associated with a particular disease or disorder.

TELEOLOGY—The philosophical viewpoint that human life and behavior, and reality in general, are dominated by purpose; also, the philosophical study of ends, purposes, and goals.

THERAPEUTIC—Pertaining to the art of healing or therapy.

TRAUMA (TRAUMATIC)—Pertaining to a wound or injury, whether physical or psychological.

TRAUMATIC NEUROSIS—A neurotic disorder that results from the threat of severe injury or death.

UNCONSCIOUS—Absence of awareness. In psychology, mental processes that are inaccessible to the person but still exert a dynamic influence on his mental life and behavior.

UTOPIA—An imaginary island described by Sir Thomas More which enjoyed the utmost perfection in government, law, and politics; hence a place or state of ideal perfection.

WORRY—Persistent nonadjustive thinking about personal problems, characterized by a strong, unpleasant emotional tone.

A SELECTIVE BIBLIOGRAPHY

Here are a few of the many books that deal with psychological problems and how to cope with them. They are all good books and well worth reading, but to help you get started we have starred a few of them because they are among the best.

Bennett, E. M., *The Search for Emotional Security*. New York: Ronald, 1959.

Brachfeld, O., *Inferiority Feelings in the Individual and the Group*. New York: Grune & Stratton, 1951.

Dodge, R. & Kahn, E., *The Craving for Superiority*. New Haven: Yale University Press, 1931.

Ellis, A., *Reason and Emotion in Psychotherapy*. New York: Lyle Stewart, 1962.

Fosdick, H. E., *On Being a Real Person*. New York: Harper, 1943.

Freeman, Lucy, & Greenwald, H., *Emotional Maturity in Love and Marriage*. New York: Harper, 1961.

*Fromm, E., *The Art of Loving*. New York: Harper, 1956.

Fromme, A., *The Psychologist Looks at Sex and Marriage*. Englewood Cliffs, N.J.: Prentice-Hall, 1950.

Garre, W. J., *Basic Anxiety*. New York: Philosophical Library, 1962.

Hope, W., *Each His Own Tyrant*. New York: Sheed & Ward, 1961.

*Horney, Karen, *Neurosis and Human Growth*. New York: Norton, 1950.

Houselander, Caryll, *Guilt*. New York: Sheed & Ward, 1951.

Hunt, M. M., *Her Infinite Variety: the American Woman as Lover, Mate and Rival*. New York: Harper, 1962.

Jersild, A., *In Search of Self*. New York: Teachers College, Columbia University, 1952.

*May, R., *Man's Search for Himself*. New York: Norton, 1953.

Mosse, E. P., *The Conquest of Loneliness*. New York: Random House, 1957.

Overstreet, H. A., *The Mature Mind*. New York: Norton, 1949.

*Saul, L. J., *Emotional Maturity*. Philadelphia: Lippincott, 1947.

————, *The Hostile Mind: The Sources and Consequences of Rage and Hate*. New York: Random House, 1956.

Schwartz, Charlene, *Neurotic Anxiety*. New York: Sheed & Ward, 1954.

*Stern, K., *The Third Revolution*. New York: Harcourt, Brace, 1954.

*Strecker, E. A., *Their Mothers' Sons*, rev. ed. Philadelphia: Lippincott, 1951.

Strecker, E. A., & Lathbury, V. T., *Their Mothers' Daughters*. Philadelphia: Lippincott, 1956.

Thouless, R., *How to Think Straight*. New York: Simon & Schuster, 1941.

Warters, J., *Achieving Maturity*. New York: McGraw-Hill, 1949.